A Hand Cart Down
HENN'S WALK

A Hand Cart Down

HENN'S WALK

The Times and Trials of an Apprentice
Carpenter and Joiner: 1959-1965

Robert Betteridge

BREWIN BOOKS

BREWIN BOOKS
19 Enfield Ind. Estate,
Redditch,
Worcestershire,
B97 6BY
www.brewinbooks.com

Published by Brewin Books 2021

A CIP catalogue record for this book is
available from the British Library.

ISBN: 978-1-85858-727-1

Printed and bound in Great Britain
by Severnprint Ltd.

Dedication

This is dedicated to the memory of James Hennessey, my apprentice, friend and colleague who was tragically taken from us too early in his life. Also to my mentors and college tutors who gave me a skill and thereby a living and security for my family.

My thanks to my wife who worked tirelessly to transcribe my writings to manuscript.

Many thanks also to Sue who both proof read the manuscript and managed to get it into some sort of order for printing.

Preface

Bob Betteridge was born in January 1944 to the accompaniment of air raid sirens in Weoley Castle, Birmingham. He was
educated at Princethorpe Junior and Infant School and
Ilmington Road Secondary Modern.

On leaving school he became an apprentice carpenter and
joiner with Midlands Electricity Board, Birmingham Area
Building and Civil Works Section. He attended Matthew
Boulton Technical College, then in Suffolk Street, and Hall
Green Technical College, where he gained City and Guilds
Intermediate and Advanced Certificates in Carpentry and
Joinery and the Full Technological Certificate in Building
Construction. In 1965 he became an Associate of the
Incorporated British Institute of Certified Carpenters.

In 1972 Bob became Foreman Carpenter and Joiner and
in 1975 General Foreman, Building and Civil Works, a
position he held in its various forms until his early retirement
after thirty-six years. During those years he was based at Piers
Road, Handsworth; Wharf Lane, Solihull and finally at
George Road, Erdington.

1

Trials And Ideals

Looking back the office was dingy and reeked of the austerity of post war Britain. The walls were distempered, the windows still had brackets on their frames which would have been the home of a black-out blind just fifteen years earlier. I sat in front of brown leather-covered desk on a none too stable chair, both of which had seen far better days.

I had plenty of time to gaze at my surroundings, for no-one asked my opinion. A battle raged around me. The protagonists were two formidable women, one who thought she knew best what I wanted and one who thought she knew what was best for me. Neither asked my opinion.

I was fifteen years old and today's generation would marvel at my lack of independence. In 1959 it was different. Most parents wanted a major input into deciding the fate of their offspring. There were compelling reasons for their concern. They and their parents had lived through deprivation, unemployment and inequality, survived world wars and at the same time witnessed the slaughter of friends, relatives and workmates. Although they worshipped Churchill's war time leadership and resolve, they had already been driven to the true ideals of socialism and trade unionism. The promise of a National Health Service, of nationalisation and thereby a Britain of social justice and uniformity. By 1959 that dream, in part, had been realised but those intervening years between wars were still branded, and unmovable from the minds of those who suffered so much.

So here we were, the school leaver's employment office in Selly Oak. One formidable lady was my mother who had been well coached by my father. The other was the employment officer, clad befitting her demeanour, in tweed. I remember she had a large circular brooch of pears, simple but attractive, on the lapel of her jacket. I had already decided that it was useless to intervene even if I had dared. My opinion, it seemed, was of little interest.

Mother had come to the interview with pre-conceived, and in my parents minds, a laudable agenda. Whatever job I had must be secure and have a pension. This I found out later was the format for any caring parent. To me and probably the employment officer a pension seemed a very, very long way off. The verbal battle centred on my elder brother who had successfully completed his apprenticeship as an electrician with the local electricity board which had given him security and a pension when, and if, he eventually reached sixty-five. My brother was to be the yard stick to which my future was to be gauged.

I had dramatically under-achieved throughout my school years, to the extent where, at my junior school I was told not to bother to take the then criteria for the bright and not so bright – the 11 plus. This decision much peeved my mother and led to a confrontation with my form teacher in the corridor outside my classroom and much embarrassment for me.

The employment officer had my academic prowess laid out before her. I would concede that it was not impressive, woodwork, technical drawing and English – the latter two by the skin of my teeth. Midlands Electricity Board were very selective and I, the employment officer made it clear, was not bright enough. Mother was adamant and wanted for me the same as my brother. Stalemate, and neither asked my opinion.

It seemed an almost eternity of my mind wandering and unconcern when a sharp "Bob, answer the lady" brought me back into the world. I confess the question had not been heard. The tweedy Civil Servant repeated when she perceived that her original question had not been comprehended or indeed heard.

"What would you like to work at Robert?" she asked.

"A carpenter," I said.

"I want him to be an electrician," interposed mother, "like his brother at the electricity board."

"A carpenter!" smirked the employment officer.

"There won't be any such trade in ten years' time."

"Electrician would be better," said my mother.

I relapsed into my depressive and mind wandering world. The discussion continued, my input now redundant and it seemed the only job I wanted was to be denied consideration by the very people who should have encouraged my genuine desire.

In 1959 there was no lottery as to whether you would be employed or not, everyone was found a job of work. Where I lived there were three major options which accounted for most of the school leavers, Cadbury's, Austin Motor Company and a selection of factories located at nearby Selly Oak. The definition of what work you would actually do was determined by that critical examination at eleven years old. If you passed that test you would go to the local grammar school and progress to a white collar job. The majority, who failed, went to a local secondary modern and became, what it termed, blue collar workers. The inequalities that existed in society meant that an assessment at eleven years of age predetermined your starting point on the economic and social ladder. What became apparent as my own career progressed was that my starting point on the ladder retarded my initial ambition.

My unconcern and lack of input into the now heated discussion between mother and the tweed clad employment officer, had reached a point where I myself robotically nodded agreement to any half heard suggestion. I looked to my left where a flushed mother showed all the tell-tale and familiar traits of a not often seen anger. Mother had lost her war of words with the tweed woman. An appointment had been arranged with a small heating, ventilation and lighting company in the city. Not Council, not Electricity Board and, in my mother eyes, no security and of course no pension. The battle for the wellbeing of her youngest son had turned to a debacle, a rout in which the tweed woman had been a formidable opponent and I a mere pawn.

Someone, I don't know who, once said "Lost battles do not necessarily amount to a lost war!" Indeed in British history such scenarios are quite common and some well within my late mother's recall. I doubt such thoughts were in her mind as we left the tweed woman's domain but mother's distain was encapsulated by her unnaturally sullen demeanour. She did not like her adversary, not one little bit. "No security and above all, no pension." Father's reaction was as expected, as my future was debated over our tea consisting of rissoles, mashed potatoes and peas as I recall. I found solace in my food, and no-one asked my opinion anyway. Mum made lovely rissoles, so it must have been a Monday.

And so it was on an early June morning Mother, followed closely by her youngest slightly reticent son, boarded a No. 20 bus from our Weoley Castle home into the city. The lighting, heating and ventilation company's premises were situated in a back alley, off a back alley, in a side street, at the rear of the late, but in my view not lamented, Bingley Hall. A location now occupied by the magnificent Symphony Hall.

Large wooden gates opened from any adjacent alley to provide vehicular access to a yard cluttered with ladders, steps, cable and various other items befitting the nature of that company's business. In the corner of the yard was what looked like an office, and from inside came the sound of voices. Mother, followed by son, picked their way through the clutter across the uneven blue brick paving to the open door. The interior was shabby, small and sparsely furnished with two chairs and two stools which had saw marks on the seats, indicating their dual use as work benches. The rectangular table was covered in newspaper which had been stained by over spill from an assorted collection of mugs and cups, most of which were chipped. The table was also the resting place of a plate with the remains of a bacon sandwich, crust and bacon rind congealing in an over exuberantly shaken pool of tomato ketchup. This was quite obviously the mess room where the labour force dined along with numerous bacteria and the local mouse population for that part of the city.

Behind the table one chair was occupied by a middle-aged, red faced man who was totally engrossed in my father's favourite newspaper, The Sporting Buff, while a stool was taken by an acned youth, not much older than me. He looked up but found us far less interesting than the sports pages of the Daily Mirror. Both were aware of our presence but made no effort to ask why we were obviously disturbing their morning break.

"Excuse me," mother impatiently rapped the dilapidated panelled door. The man behind the table slowly looked over the top of his glasses and then over the top of his Sporting Buff.

"What can I do for you love?" he droned.

Mother was far from impressed, twitched her shoulders and tapped her food on the worn linoleum floor covering in a strikingly irritated pose. Her obvious ire was not lost on either owner of the The Buff or the reader of the Mirror who tucked the paper into the pocket of a dirty blue overall pocket and squeezed through the doorway passed mother and out into the yard. The Buff now lay, double spread on the table, and the crimson faced rose to his full height of about 5' 2".

"This is my son," she announced. "He is here for an interview for the post of apprentice electrician, our appointment is at 10.15 am and we are five minutes early." The crimson one looked perplexed.

"Gaffer's not here at the moment," he said, rather nervously, folding The Buff to its normal size.

"Will he be long?" asked an even more agitated mother.

"He has gone to Tipton, missis, to price a job. He told me not to expect him back," there was a long pause, "until tomorrow." He looked down at the now expertly folded Buff, "must have forgotten I suppose."

I doubt that mother heard the apology that followed, for she had seen and heard quite enough by then. A short trot saw me catch her up. We walked down Suffolk Street in silence to where waited, at the terminus at Holiday Street, a No. 20 bus. Mother ignored our stop and turned the corner into Navigation Street and the terminus for the Bristol Road buses.

"Where are we going mum?" I said, although I had a sneaking feeling that I knew the answer.

"To see that woman," said mother. I was right, the mood mother was in could result in the capitulation of 'Tweeds'. The fiasco had given her a very definite advantage.

I didn't witness the ensuing confrontation, only the icy greeting that was exchanged outside the 'Tweeds' office. They were ensconced inside and I found myself outside the door that had closed as I was about to follow the warring factions inside. I suppose most school boys in their time in education have found themselves excluded from a class for some mis-demeanour or the other. I was no exception and felt exactly as I did on those occasions and I tried to hear what was going on inside. Mother eventually emerged, her demeanour changed and with a countenance that exuded quiet satisfaction.

Two days later, in the post, came an invitation to attend an interview at the Education and Training Section of Midlands Electricity Board in Dale End in the city. The news of my forthcoming interview for secure and pensioned employment was greeted with euphoria by family and close friends. It was, of course, mother's tenacity that had won the interview. I appreciated what she had done for me but was less than confident of a successful outcome to my interview, for no matter how hard I tried I could not be enthused over a future as an electrician.

The Midlands Electricity Board Birmingham Area Offices were located in Dale End, the main body of the building being a former shopping arcade, YMCA building and the area around a major sub-station. The Education and Training Section being in the former galleried shopping arcade, which despite its rather rundown appearance I can now appreciate as architecturally very Edwardian and, in its heyday, must have been beautiful. The whole effect was spoiled by an under ceiling of galvanised chicken wire which had been suspended across the arcade for its length. This was obviously done to protect the public from falling glass from the multitude of glazing in the roof above. No doubt this protection was installed during the war years.

At the time of nationalisation of electricity in 1948, office space in the city would have been at a premium due to the heavy bombing raids which destroyed many buildings in the city centre. This, I would suggest, would be why the electricity board had found itself, in part, installed in this unused accommodation.

Mr. White, who I later learned was known to all by the unimaginative nickname of 'Chalky', was a small dapper man. His black hair was generously Brylcreemed with a precise parting which would have been victorious in any ploughing contest. He wore a navy blue double-breasted blazer, with a Boy Scout Association badge proudly emblazoned on his breast pocket, which was also the home of an immaculately pressed white handkerchief. A club tie of differing coloured diagonal bars, knotted to perfection within the collar of a whiter than white shirt. I suspect with his status of Education and Training Officer that protocol prevented him from wearing a rakish cravat which was highly fashionable at the time, particularly with a blazer. His office was in one of the former shops on the gallery of the arcade. He had seated me directly facing him across a desk that bore testament to an ultra-tidy mind. My mother was seated to my left and slightly behind me. She was silent and completely at ease having been charmed by 'Chalky' on our arrival. Yes, I thought, 'Chalky' could have been a real matinee idol. A Niven, Colman or Fairbanks. He oozed 'pass the sick bucket' charm and confidence. I was nervous but strangely not ill at ease, although his lady killer charm did not extend to the junior mail clerk, also in attendance, and this aspiring employee. The ensuing interview was full of surprises, some unwelcome. This

8

interview, unlike the ones with 'Tweeds', was conducted with me rather than mother. Indeed, her presence was purely coincidental. I know how mother must have felt.

"Just some little tests," said 'Chalky' his eyes glinting like a barn owl's at night, through the then trendy horn-rimmed spectacles. Oh dear, I didn't think that tests were involved. My mind flitted back to junior school and my lack of ability that meant my non-involvement in the 11 plus exams.

"Bit of arithmetic and some English," 'Chalky' leaned over his desk and handed me a sheet of paper and a pencil. The arithmetic was, I was surprised to see, just within my capabilities and while 'Chalky' talked to mother I answered, only just within the scheduled time, all ten questions. He then handed me an English paper which I was also able to conclude again within the time allowed by 'Chalky's' wristwatch.

A glimpse to my left confirmed that mother was obviously satisfied by my achievement. No-one was more surprised than I. 'Chalky' proceeded with an interrogation which became more in-depth as we progressed. All questions were addressed to me and mother's input was nil. Eventually, 'Chalky' who had been writing copious notes, rested his fountain pen on the desk.

"Robert, what do you want to be, truthfully?" I felt I had to be honest. I was waiting for mother to say "An electrician like his brother with security and a pension." Mother was silent and my answer seemed an eternity leaving my lips.

"A carpenter," I said. 'Chalky' leaned back in his chair. There was a discernible intake of breath from mother's direction, but nothing was said.

"I was under the impression," said 'Chalky', "that you wished to become an electrician." I waited, in vain, for maternal input, but again mother remained silent.

"I have also wanted to be a carpenter sir," I replied.

'Chalky' looked across at my mother.

"John has done quite well and is out of his apprenticeship," he was referring to my older brother.

"We thought Bob would want to follow him," said mother. She looked downcast, security, pension and all.

"We do happen to have a vacancy for an apprentice carpenter and joiner in our Building and Civil Works Section, would you be interested in taking up that vacancy for a trial period of six months?" asked 'Chalky'.

A voice behind me said "Yes."

'Chalky' ignored the affirmative from mother, at the same time giving her a starfish glance and adding "Robert".
I could not believe my ears, an electricity board with a building section and carpenters and joiners.

"Yes, please," I replied with obvious enthusiasm.

An overjoyed mother was busy thanking 'Chalky' but could not resist.

"I think job security and a pension are very important, don't you Mr. White?"

"Very much so Mrs. Betteridge!" said 'Chalky' shaking her hand. "That's someway off, but we must all start somewhere," he chuckled and ushered us out of his office to an outer room where his waiting lackey filled in details. Please mum, I thought, don't mention security and a pension again, she didn't.

2

From Frying Pan To Fire?

Mid July brought my last few days at secondary modern school. It was indeed a strange few days for all of my fellow scholars already had employment awaiting them. Numbers in my year had already been much depleted, for the majority had left at either Christmas or Easter. This shortage of pupils in the last year had meant that virtually all of the remaining were elevated to prefects. Some who would not have even been considered for this accolade found themselves belatedly favoured. All of us felt, however, 'demob' happy and could not wait to venture forth from school, known affectionately as Ilmington College of Knowledge to a job of work and a wage. So it was just two weeks before my employment was due to commence I walked, for the last time, through the wrought iron gates of my school towards my employment.

It is strange that friendships, some ten years old, suddenly and abruptly terminated at this point in time and were never rekindled. Children you have shared virtually every day of every year of your school life are lost in the realisation that adult hood and a new life awaits. I remember meeting a school friend at an airport in Corfu, some forty years from the last time I saw him on my last day at school. I recognised him for he was always the tallest in my year. It only needed my name to instigate his memory of me. Our conversation was curtailed by the urgency of boarding our respective aircraft. I always regretted that we could not have had a real walk down memory lane. He moved some twenty years ago a long way from Brum, so it seems unlikely I will ever see him again. By and large my school years were happy, apart from swimming lessons! I suppose there are many of my ilk who wonder just what happened to so many friends associated with those years.

"You don't know where you are going and I don't want you late on your first day!" The letter had arrived.

I had to report to the Midlands Electricity Board (Birmingham Area Building and Civil Works Section) Piers Road, Handsworth, Birmingham at 8.00 am prompt on 10th August, 1959, to a Mr. Reginald Wamsley (Foreman Carpenter and Joiner). Mother was explaining the need for a dummy run as a guide to me finding my new employment and assessing how long the journey would take. As a consequence two days later I was forced from my slumbers at 5.00 in the morning, I had only previously seen 5.00 in the evening. I was roused by my father who woke at that time every morning, even at weekends! He started work at 6.00 am at nearby Cadbury and had done so for thirty years excluding war service. Dad and mum had no idea where Handsworth was.

"Never been that side of town," they had said, almost in unison.

As a result of my early rising, and ensuing nocturnal badgering, I found myself with a small group of early starters at my local bus stop, city bound. It was 6.00 am. A neighbour, leaning against the telephone box adjacent to the bus stop, inhaled his first cigarette which was the forerunner to a bout of hacking coughs. The attack ended.

"Hello young Bob, where are you off to then, a day trip?"
"No, Mr. Lawton, I have to go to Handsworth to find where I

have to start work." He took another deep drag of a fast shortening cigarette, frowned under the angled peak of his flat cap.

"Handsworth, that's a long way!" he said.

The bus arrived, its destination board still prefixed by a NS, which indicated it had seen duty on the Night Service. A bleary eyed conductor was leaning against the stairs to the upper deck. Every working day travellers exchanged 'Morning's' their common bond being the timing of this particular Birmingham City Transport Corporation Bus.

A brief moment elapsed before the bus conductor reached over and rang twice for the bus to depart. On the platform was a buxom lady, panting and gasping, having broken into a trot of many moving parts. The lady I knew worked at the Accident Hospital. I had witnessed her short, but exhausting run from the window of my upstairs seat. The atmosphere on the upper deck in a time when virtually every male smoked, either cigarettes or pipe, was akin to a thick smog. It was considerably worse in the winter months when it was deemed a cardinal sin to slide open a window. The oddity of a non-smoker, like myself, was not catered for on the upper deck and if passive smoking, an unheard of hazard then, was an active ingredient to a premature death, then I should have met my demise years ago!

I suppose it was no surprise that my journey into the city, about thirty minutes, was punctuated with periods of token sleep caused entirely by the unearthly hour. I stirred to consciousness in Bath Row at the bus stop outside the Accident Hospital and Davenport's Brewery in time to see the buxom woman alight, saying 'Goodbye's' to all and sundry. The driver and conductor had changed at Harborne, the new crew had been waiting near the bus garage, opposite Princes

Corner, and they replaced bleary eyes and his mate. A short time later the No. 20 bus pulled into its terminus in Suffolk Street.

I now had to cross the city to Livery Street where the buses for Handsworth and the north-western environs terminated, adjacent to Snow Hill. This walk I knew well. I had often, when train spotting, criss-crossed from Birmingham's main stations, New Street and Snow Hill, in the quest to see locomotives of both regions, LMS and GWR. Navigation Street, Stephenson Street, Temple Street, St. Philip's Churchyard and Colmore Row, where the impressive façade of the Great Western Hotel housed the entrance to the architecturally proud Snow Hill Station. The change of stations was also a bind for travellers. Service men could often be seen humping their kit between the two locations. The trek from New Street Station was worse because of the steep incline of Temple Street. The city's chaotic and congested one-way system meant that a taxi would often take much longer than the irksome foot transfer. I have heard that porters at both stations could make a few bob assisting desperate, weary and bemused rail passengers to overcome this formidable change of station.

A multitude of buses awaited my choice, all of which went past my intended destination. The beautiful blue and cream adorning West Bromwich Corporation transport in tandem with the more sombre blue and cream of the city's buses. They took the same route out of the city, Snow Hill, Constitution Hill, Great Hampton Street, Hockley Hill, Soho Road and onwards to a whole variety of destinations within and beyond Birmingham's boundaries. Even in 1959 however, the route taken by these buses was beset by congestion problems, alleviated to some extent by the later construction of the

Hockley Flyover. This removed the traffic shambles which dogged Hockley but made worse the rush hour chaos along Soho Road and, into the city, Great Hampton Street. Passing years have seen this arterial route worsen to one single slow moving block of traffic and a headache for the unsuspecting, especially in mornings and evenings.

However, at 6.45 am no such problems existed and I selected a No. 70, Oxhill Road, as my mode of convenience. I sat on the side seat, near the platform, for an easy access if my stop was missed.

"Piers Road please," I said to conductress.

"Whereabouts that, son?"

"I am not sure," I said, "I know it's off the Soho Road."

"Anyone know Piers Road?" she addressed a sparsely populated lower deck.

"Yes," said a woman's voice towards the front of the bus. "Put him off at the Ivy House Pub, it's just back from the stop."

"That's 4d," said the conductress. "I'll give you a call."

The journey was interesting and I was engrossed rather like tourists, in a town completely new to them, you see gazing trance like from coach windows.

"Next one's yours son." It was the woman up the bus.

"Yours love," echoed the conductress. I rose from my seat and swung to the platform, holding tight to the chromium plated pole. I nodded my thanks to the conductress and alighted onto a wide pavement. It was just after 7.00 am.

I walked back some fifty yards towards the city and there was Piers Road. Piers Road was no more than 200 yards long. Fifty yards down, facing a small Junior and Infant School, were a large pair of wooden gates painted green. The right hand one had a wicket gate incorporated into its construction. Both main gates and wicket were heavily padlocked. The gates which bore MEB insignia were hung from two large brick piers, each with an ornamental stone capping. I later wondered if those fine brick piers were instrumental in the naming of the road. I was standing absorbing the location when I was startled by a call from the gates of the school opposite.

"They won't be open until half past seven son." It was the caretaker of the school. "You can try the other entrance."

"Oh right," I said, "where is that?"

"By the bus stop round the corner on Soho Road." He replied.

"Thanks," I said and walked back into Piers Road and to the bus stop I had just left. There, back of pavement, was an ornate but very strong wrought iron gate. On the gate was a plaque bearing the words Electricity Supply. The gate was locked. A steep path of blue paving ran down for about seventy yards to a complex of buildings. This was obviously the foot access and I studied the buildings for some time and then crossed the road to catch the bus to the city centre and thence to home.

I arrived home at 8.30 am and mother was surprised to see me.

"Have you been?" said mum. "It didn't take long."

"No mum, I went far too early."

"Oh well, I don't know that side of town."

"No mum, neither do I but I am learning."

August 10th was a lovely summer's day. I woke at 6.15 am and came down stairs, mother was in the kitchen.

"I have done you sandwiches and put a nice piece of cake for you." A flask stood on the table. "I've done you a nice drop of tea as well."

The flask was being packed into a khaki shoulder bag which was stamped inside the flap 'US Army'. The bag had been purchased from an Army and Navy store in Selly Oak. It was symbolic of one of three items that will be eternally associated with the blue collar manual worker of post war Britain, the other two being his Daily Mirror and the woodbine cigarette that drooped from almost every working man's lips. By 1959 the flat cap, still prominent with the older worker, was not finding favour with the younger set, mainly because it became fashionable to style their hair to match any popular singer of the day. Whereas a cap and a regimental short back and sides went together like faggots and peas, Cross and Blackwell or Accles and Pollocks. The shoulder bag was akin to the white collar worker's brief case. Indeed I once carried out a straw poll of brief case carriers and found there were common factors. The both were a conveyance for lunch, both carried a piece of fruit, an apple for manual and a banana for white collar, with the Daily Express the most popular choice with office workers. The younger set of both groupings were partial to Smith's Crisps, the one with the separate salt bag, which appear to have been going for years and years. Those white collar workers who smoked went for Players and if they wanted to be a bit flash, Craven A.

In a simplistic way this quaint piece of Sociology (did such a science exist in 1959?) defines working and lower middle class. Anyway, I had no doubt of my standing in society as I slung my lunch bag over my shoulder and set off at a smart pace for the bus stop and the 6.45 am No. 20. On this my first day of work, I looked the very epitome of the working class lad. I was hoping that someone would ask me where Handsworth was, but no-one did.

I arrived at my Handsworth bus stop at 7.40 am, still 20 minutes before my required attendance at 8.00 am. The beautiful wrought iron entrance gate was closed but a large galvanised padlock hung loosely from a thick chain indicating the site open for business. I opened the gate tentatively and stepped onto the blue paved path that steeply descended to the cluster of buildings at the bottom of the slope. The gate clicked to closure behind me, this was it – no turning back now.

3

Formal Introductions

So it was, with a mixture of excitement and trepidation that I stood, hesitantly, in front of the double doors that were enclosed within an entrance hallway which opened into the interior of the complex. I ventured forth and again hesitated at the bottom of a flight of stairs leading to the first floor from whence distance voices and laughter could be heard.

At the top of the stairs there suddenly appeared a man in his early 60s. His flat checked cap pulled tight to his head, the press stud on the peak only just keeping the separation of peak and top. His features were craggy and he had a Cromwellian wart on the bridge of his nose that would have made the wearing of spectacles an impossibility. His blue bib and brace straps cut into a thick roll neck jumper. This was Bill, the yard labourer.

"Looking for someone son?" he enquired.

"Yes sir," I said, "I have to see a Mr. Wamsley, the carpenter and joiner foreman."

Bill smiled. It was probably the only time in his life that he had been referred to as 'sir' and we became good friends.

"You one of the new lads then?"

"Yes," I said, still at the bottom of the stairs.

"Come on up then, what's your name?"

"Bob," I replied, quickly adding "Sir."

"I'm Bill," adding, "from now on" and chuckled.

Bill poked his head round an office door.

"Reg, one of your new lads is here." Bill nodded in response to the instruction from within. "Come with me lad, the boss will see you in a bit."

I followed Bill along a corridor to a large end room full of oddments of chairs and tables and men in brown, white and blue overalls and filled with the blue haze of cigarette smoke. The generated noise was indeed a happy one with shouting, laughter and lots of swearing. This was the mess room. Bill gave me a chair and I sat down. I was bemused, I had never witnessed such a scene. Although I knew enough to know from my father's and brother's love of horse and dog racing that much of the heated conversation ranged around the subject of betting, of football, of cricket, of boxing and any other sporting activity.

"Cup of tea, Bob?" Bill awoke me from my fascination.

"Yes please," I said.

The tea arrived in a large white, cracked mug – tea with a hint of milk! It was strong, very strong but, as I later found out, the only way it should be made and imbibed by those who would work within any of the building trades. Now I hate tea made in any other way.

I looked across to the opposite wall where a large clock with Roman numerals and a dusty mahogany case chimed 8.00 am. Those assembled in the room rose like automatons, folding newspapers and draining mugs of their contents, departing the room still gossiping and laughing, leaving just Bill and I. Bill gathered the mugs and emptied the dregs into a large Belfast sink, swilled them under a cold tap and left them inverted on a wooden draining board. Chairs resumed their allotted space, tables cleared, ash trays emptied and replaced. Then Bill nodded.

"See you later son," and he too left.

A short time elapsed before a stocky man in a light weight fawn jacket, a scarlet face and blinky eyes stood before me. His flame red hair losing its unequal struggle with the grey of the aging process.

"Are you Robert Betteridge?" he asked. I was already at attention.

"Yes Mr. Wamsley, sir," I replied.

"Mr. Wamsley will do son," he said, as I handed him my letter of introduction. "You have made a good start," he remarked. "You were early and you found us. Weoley Castle is a long way, let's hope you keep it up."

I soon learnt that punctuality was treated very seriously. I was pleased that I had made a trial run and a good first impression.

"Right, follow me lad."

I went off in hot pursuit of my foreman who moved at a surprising pace. His short legs moving with the rapidity of bees wings. Doors closed on me as I tried to keep up and I was pleased when we eventually reached our destination.

"Morning Harold, morning Maurice," greeted Mr. Wamsley.

"Morning Reg," the duo replied in unison. "This is Robert, my new lad, kit him and give me a ring when you've done. See you in a bit." Said my mentor and as quick as we arrived, he was gone.

"What do we call you, Robert or Bob?" asked the one I guessed was Maurice.

"Bob please," I replied.

I decided to drop the 'Sir' and therefore the ingrained and expected term of address of my school days.

"Full name?" said a voice behind me. It was Harold. I complied. "Spell it, just the Betteridge part." I again complied.

He continued to fill in an index card, at the same time instructing Maurice.

"Two pair brown bib and brace, two overall jackets, two standard towels. Chest size?" I shook my head. "Inside leg?" again I shook my head. "Have a guess Maurice!" Maurice did, and when I put the trousers on I never thought my feet would come out the other end.

"Bit shorter Maurice," said Harold.

Maurice's guess with the jacket left me so lacking movement in my upper body any work would have been out of the question. Eventually, and after squeezing into a pair of overalls that made me look like Rudolf Nureyev on a good day, a fitment was found near to my size.

"Looks a picture, doesn't he Maurice?"

"He certainly does Harold." I blushed and they laughed.

"Every inch a chippy," said Maurice.

"Every inch," said Harold. "New kit every twelve months, try not to lose them. No white aprons in stock at the moment." Harold picked up the phone.

"Hello Reg, we have given him a going over, he is all yours."

Harold and Maurice grinned like a pair of Cheshire cats. That was the stores and I was pleased when my foreman arrived at his now familiar machine gun pace. The stores office, Harold, Maurice and all, was a separate entity of half-glazed wooden panels and false ceiling, within a much larger area.

Holding tightly to my new overalls, jackets, towels and my haversack, I desperately struggled in the wake of my foreman who uttered no word or bothered to check that I was still in tow. The area containing the stores was full of racking, containing numerous types of sheet materials: plywood, plasterboard, Formica and such, with other storage areas dedicated to scaffolding. A table, covered in green felt, with a large T-square and separate unit containing sheets of glass, occupied one corner. At the far end of the room was a metal stair case which rose to a door and a balcony. Reg was already ascending those stairs, I hurried and just managed to grab the door before it closed on me. Reg made his way a further 20 feet to another door, despite dropping my towels, I managed to enter the room just behind him. He took a couple of paces inside and then turned.

"This is the Joiner's Shop," he announced.

The workshop was quite long with twelve work benches in a row, against an external wall with a window at the end of each bench. A smaller square room with very large windows housing comparatively small panes was at the end of the larger room. It had two work benches and contained a clutter of completed joinery works waiting for a painter's attention: doors, gates and a range of boxes and cabinets.

Only two benches, half way along the larger room, were occupied and I followed Reg to those benches.

"Morning Bert, morning Bill. Where's Ray?"

"Down in the mill," replied Bert.

"Good, I thought he'd gone missing again," said Reg.

"This is Mr. Boyce and that's Mr. Turner, this is Bob," said Reg.

Both men smiled and acknowledge my "hello". I remember thinking that they were of an advanced age, as indeed they were, well into their 60s. Both wore shirts with detachable collars and smartly knotted ties. No overalls, but white joiner's aprons. A lad in brown overalls appeared at the top of another flight of stairs, which by the sound of machines whirring below us, descended to the mill. The lad, who I guessed was about 17 bade Reg a "morning". Reg glowered back.

"Were you on time this morning?"

The lad was Ray. He flushed slightly.

"10 to," he said.

Reg nodded in my direction.

"This is Bob. Tell him all he needs to know and put him straight on his duties."

"You will be working in the Joiners Shop for a few weeks under these two gentlemen. Mr. Boyce is in charge of the workshop, you report to him."

Reg departed, rapidly exiting through the door which had been our entrance.

Bert nodded in the direction of the workbench next to his own.

"That's your bench, son," he said.

"Get your overalls and Ray will sort you out a locker for your coat, towels and spare pair of overalls."

I followed Ray to the end of the workshop and a row of about twenty green metal lockers. Ray found an empty one.

"That's yours," he said.

None of the lockers appeared to be locked or able to be locked. I need not have been concerned.

Bert had not moved from behind his bench but when he did it was obvious that he was in some pain and walked with a severe limp. Sustained pain was etched on his face but I never ever heard him complain. Along with many others of Bert's age, in any of the building trades, arthritis was an abundant and disabling curse. More of that later, for a chapter that relates the gross abuse of building workers and the corruptive influence of harsh uncaring employers in the first half of the 20th century, influenced deeply my political leanings. Many of my mentors bore the mental and physical scars of that period and when the time was right would graphically relate that period of time to me.

Initial introductions complete, new overalls resplendent, it really was time to get to work and the first tentative steps of my five year apprenticeship, not only in my chosen craft, but also in life itself.

4

Duties To Be Done

Having returned to my allotted bench Bert instructed Ray to 'sort me out'. It was approaching 10.00 am which, as I was to learn, was the first break of the day, for ten minutes. Ray had drawn up a list of my responsibilities, which fell to the youngest apprentice to perform. So, when I was around it was I who carried out the traditional and time honoured tasks that were many and varied, and sometimes beyond the call.

I had never made a cup of tea in my short life and I must admit that the thought of making tea three times a day for up to seventeen hard bitten carpenters and joiners, filled me with abject fear. Ray though was a great teacher and he taught me well, just as he had been tutored by his peers. At this juncture I feel that it is right to enlighten those who are interested just what those duties were.

Firstly, I would be expected to be at work no later than 7.45 am, although 8.00 am was my official starting time. My first duty would be to make sure that the cast iron glue pots were topped up and the outer pot, that contained water to heat the glue, was full. The actual glue was animal based and was crystallised into rectangles, about 6" by 4" and approximately ¼" thick. They were broken up by wrapping them in cloth and smashing, with a hammer, into small pieces. Heated by the boiling water the pieces became a thick amber liquid. The pots had to be checked frequently when they were in use for if they boiled dry the smell was appalling and the lad in charge was the subject of derision and abuse. It happened to me but once – the first and last time.

The large white enamel jug of tea had to be available to all who wanted it by 7.50 am and, of course, the apprentice was the maker. At 9.30 am it was a duty to ask all working in the Joiners Shop if they wanted anything from the local shop. Most times the answer was no but occasionally I would have to fetch a sandwich from the local café or a newspaper. The foreman brickie would sometimes ask me to get him a London printed Daily Express. I was told he had a fetish to bet on greyhounds running at the London tracks and would invest in the selections of that newspaper. His surname was Trigger and, as one wag suggested, you would have thought his forte would have been horses!

The next official break was at 1.00 pm, for thirty minutes. At twenty-two minutes to that hour I would ask again if anything was needed from the local shops. I would then prepare tea for the occupants of the Joiners Shop. The final break of the working day was at 3.00 pm and involved just tea making. The 'lad' was in charge also of the replenishment of the resources for that beverage namely, tea, sugar and milk. The only acceptable teas were Brook Bond and Typhoo and you would dare not run out of any of the necessary elements.

I mentioned earlier that punctuality was very important. I was never late. We had to clock in and the clock was a circular band which was graduated into allotted numbers dedicated to each member of staff, mine was 186. When arriving at work you would turn a leaver to your number and punch a card which recorded your time of arrival. It was expensive to be late. Up to fifteen minutes late you lost a quarter of an hour's pay, up to thirty minutes late and you lost half an hour's pay. If you were over thirty minutes late you had an hour's pay deducted from your wage. If you were an hour or more late, unless you had a very good reason, you would be sent home with no pay for that day.

Ray, who was an excellent tradesman for his years, was a very poor timekeeper. I really liked Ray for it was he who saved me so much anguish in performing the demanding intricacies of my early days as an apprentice. His poor punctuality was often his demise and eventually he left before completing his apprenticeship. I can remember one morning break when Ray was sat with his feet up on a saw bench. One of the blokes asked:

"What you got on under your trousers lad?"

Ray blushed, they were his pyjamas:

"I was late and never had time to take them off!"

I asked Ray how long I would have to continue to do my apprentice chores.

"You are an apprentice until you are 21," he said.

That seemed a very long time away. He added:

"It falls to the youngest apprentice in the shop, there will be others like you."

And there were, thank goodness but January 5th 1965 seemed an awful long time away.

5

Near Enough Is Not Right,
Right Is Near Enough!
(In Work and Ethics)

The two entities of my apprenticeship were carpentry and joinery. The difference between those two components is essentially that joinery work is undertaken within a Joiners Shop and entailed the manufacture of items such as doors and frames, gates, cabinet making and the construction of shop fittings as well as a whole range of smaller items that would form the basis of this part of my training. The carpentry work would be the greater part of my apprenticeship but only marginally. The jobs would be many and very varied and could be anywhere within the Birmingham area of Midland's Electricity Board, an area which included a large slice of Warwickshire. The maintenance of some 5,000 sub-stations was a high priority as was the upkeep of seven large depots, offices, workshops and around 35 retail outlets.

However, my starting point was the Joiners Shop. I soon found that a very high standard was to be achieved and why I was to occupy the work bench adjacent to Bert's. It was impossible to be out of Bert and Bill's vision. Thus I quickly learned and digested every bit of advice they gave for I had the greatest of respect for their standards and what they tried to impart. Every day at that bench was a challenge, every day a learning process of work ethics that would be with me all of my life. They never once derided my questioning or failed to offer advice when it was plain that I was in difficulties.

The title of this chapter, 'near enough is not right, right is near enough' was instilled into every task I undertook and always under the watchful eyes of Bert and Bill. It was not only work principle that was taught but also a strong moral code. Bad language was frowned on by my mentors within the Joiners Shop. A complete and unspoken trust between my fellow woodworkers prevailed, which was the reasoning for the absent padlocks on our personal lockers. Tools could be left on work benches without fear of them being stolen. For as Bert would reason – 'what greater sin than to deprive a man of the means to feed his family.' I never knew of any acts of theft of that type in my years as a carpenter and joiner.

Of all the ethics that were expounded by my peers, by far their deep routed and unswerving belief in socialism, the co-operative movement and trade unionism had the greatest effect on my own thinking. Bert and Bill as well as other of my colleagues were very much of the traditional wing of socialism which encompassed a suspicion of all things capitalist, a hatred of the conservative party and contempt for the liberals. Bert mistrusted those who sat in the middle of politics:

"Can't be trusted," he would say. "You are either red or blue!"

Their philosophy even determined the choice of newspapers they purchased. The long gone Daily Herald, and of course the Daily Mirror were the standard choice, the Daily Mail and the Daily Express were conspicuously absent.

It was not long, therefore, that their elegant indoctrination saw me signing up to a trade union, the Amalgamated Society of Woodworkers, a decision that I have never regretted, a decision which gave me encouragement to question ideals and principles and realise just why my mentors had set their political beliefs in stone. To appreciate those beliefs it is necessary to realise the implications for my aged mentors of having being apprentice when labour was cheap, skills unappreciated but recognised that those skills were worth money to employers. There is no doubt that builders unscrupulously profited from the craftsmen they employed. Their hold purely that of job security and thereby support of their families. Society accepted the various social stratas that perpetuated a class system that very few challenged, an acceptance of a hierarchy and a predetermined part in the social structure. Know your place, and therefore your lot in life.

Apprentices had particularly hard times in an industry where injury and loss of life was high and worse considered acceptable. At the end of their apprenticeship a job was not automatic indeed the sack was the norm, for this once prized asset had grown to maturity in mind, body and craft. Only inexperience, and the over-riding factor that an employer had to now pay a full rate, saw the newly fledged unceremoniously ousted on reaching 21 years of age. That was an accepted stark reality.

Two other factors had blighted their lives – a world war and, when that had ended, a worldwide depression. Most of my elderly mentors had survived a horrific and classless slaughter in a war to end all wars. They should have returned to a promised land, fit for heroes. Twenty years later a new war of even larger and of more horrific proportions had started and the interim years had failed the heroes in a morass of unemployment and deprivation.

It was, however, a period in which labour itself realised its true worth, its value to society and its value in the market place. The early routes of socialism and the trade union movement had blossomed and now had the nous and clout to really make a difference. That era was hallowed ground to Bert, Bill, old Horace and others. They had overcome the fear of violent death at the hands of an enemy, they had put behind them the fear of the unscrupulous employer and they had been in the vanguard of those seeking even a modicum of equality and social reform.

I did, at first, have difficulty with one aspect of their teachings. The role played by the Church of England in suppressing the aspirations of the ordinary working man at the later part of the 19th Century and up to the Second World War. It was not until some thirty years later that I found the reasoning for their contempt of the church in the iconic book by Robert Tressell, The Ragged Trousered Philanthropists, which detailed the contempt for those who toiled with their hands, exercised by and perpetuated by state, church and shameless employers. The church was instrumental in trying to outlaw publication of Tressell's book which was highly critical of their role in the suppression of the working class.

So Bert, Bill and the others became deserved heroes in my eyes. Wonderful champions who were passing to my hands a craft evolved over thousands of years but also principles which I have never forgotten, fair-play, pride, respect, the satisfaction of a job well done and the means to make a living. Near enough is not right, right is near enough, an edict of our Joiners Shop, but an edict which can easily be applied to so many circumstances in life itself.

The Joiners Shop was challenging and also sometimes claustrophobic. This was particularly so when just Bert, Bill and myself were ensconced therein. Carpenters and Joiners had their break at the end of their allotted benches and thereby did not avail themselves of the raucous activity that took place on most days in the general mess room at lunchtime. Bert and Bill would often nod off at lunchtime, their heads bobbing on their chests, newspapers enveloped between their knees. They woke with automatic precision at 1.30 pm precisely to the starting up of woodworking machinery in the mill below the carpenters shop. I would often walk around the substantial parcel of land, which not only housed offices and workshops, but was also the site of a large sub-station. The whole was bounded by Piers Road, Soho Road; a council works yard of equal size to our own and two railway lines, one a branch which ran to an oil storage depot in Hockley, and one that ran into New Street Station from the North of the city. It was sometimes a relief when other carpenters were in the workshop for it was then the banter, the debates and discussions would flow. The range of subjects was enormous and everyone was allowed to develop a point of view.

Relief from the joinery facet was never far away however, for both new and maintenance works on offices, substations and shops around the area covered by MEB was a major aspect of our employment and those journeys of discovery sometimes lasted up to a month or more.

6

Transports Of Delight

The title of the chapter is somewhat of a misnomer, for transport for the whole of the Building Section of the Midlands Electricity Board comprised of two cars for use by engineers, two small vans shared between five foremen, two of which could not drive, and three Bedford lorries. In 1959 just two carpenters and joiners out of seventeen and three apprentices, could actually drive. Our foreman, Reg, he of aforementioned hectic pace, was a non-driver. Two of the three charge-hands could, Bert being the exception.

Works were surveyed by one of the charge-hands when they could grab transport or Reg if he could get a lift. Materials were delivered to sites by the charge-hands or by lorries. Job details were issued to carpenters and then it was 'shanks's pony' and public transport, which for the apprentice included carrying the tools. Of all the trades a carpenter's bag or box contains perhaps the most diverse array of tools – and the heaviest.

This chapter will introduce you to some wonderful individual, knowledgeable, humorous, caring and much respected colleagues, to whom I owe so much from a period of my working life that was probably the most rewarding. At this juncture it is probably worth reflecting upon my earning capacity. My first week's wages were £2.7s (£2.35) however, having worked a week in hand to achieve this sum; Reg took me to one side and said he was sorry, not for the amount, but because I had been over paid by 4s. (20p)! As a dutiful son I had taken my first week's wages home intact. I asked my mother how much she wanted. She asked how much I had received, when told I remember her words well.

"If I were you son, I would keep that for your bus fares!"

This was very perceptive of mother, for bus fares took quite a bit of my wage and, although an expenses and travel time structure was in place, recompense was a week in hand also.

Although it was real adventure to travel to the far outposts of the area we covered, bus fares were quite an incursion into my meagre, disposable income. There was also a big reliance on bus conductors to remember to tell you when you reached your destination. The Midland Red conductors were really good but the volume of passengers and the various distractions that Birmingham Corporation conductors had to contend with meant that specific travellers could be forgotten. Passing the disembarkation stop was a common occurrence within the city boundaries. For that tingling feeling there was nothing quite like the depressive Midland Red bus station in the city waiting to catch the first bus to Dorridge or Four Oaks, quite often the only passenger until well into the journey, clutching a piece of paper with Reg's travel directions scrawled on it. Fields of corn, cattle and grazing horses made a significant difference to the rush hour in central Birmingham.

It was very easy to empathise with the Saturday night Mystery Trips, very popular with coach companies at that time before the advent of the family car with evening outings to Stratford, Evesham, Malvern and the likes. My only concern, however, was the hope that I would meet up with my appointed mentor at the correct location and on time. Quite often that meeting would actually take place on the bus, for nearly everyone travelled by public transport in those days and punctuality was revered at Midland Electricity Board Building Section.

Foreman, Reg Wamsley, had worked for the section since the 1920s, when it was part of the City of Birmingham Electricity Supply Department; his father had also been an employee. Reg was a walking encyclopaedia on not only the locations of sub-stations, of MEB and offices but also bus services, stage locations and city centre terminus points. Quite often during the working day we would be required out at other locations from our Piers Road base. We would be called into the office where Reg would give a resume of required works, location and his own revenue saving way of reaching that destination. His way almost inevitably involved a substantial amount of walking for Reg treated the MEB coffers as if they were his own, very fiscally!

Plastic tokens of various colours and denominations were issued for bus fares. Reg's format to save money meant leaving the bus at the nearest previous stage point. I soon learnt that it was prudent to pay the extra penny or so out of my own pocket if you didn't wish to arrive on site, tools and all, completely knackered and needing time to recover. The frugal management of MEB money did not impress my work colleagues who would, out of respect, listen attentively to the 'City of Birmingham bus timetable according to Reg Wamsley', and then do their own thing. The satisfaction on Reg's face though was something to behold and reminiscent of the countenance displayed by a Chancellor of the Exchequer holding up his red dispatch box on Budget Day. For me it was a wonderful way to discover the city and its environs. By the end of my apprenticeship, I had a good geographical knowledge, after almost thirty-six years' service that knowledge was expansive.

From a practical and economic standpoint, such interim travel between jobs in today's overwhelmingly mobilised society would not be considered. In 1959 few building tradesmen could drive, and as for car ownership, wage packets certainly would not extend to such a luxury for some years to come.

So it was that yours truly could be seen humping the tools of his trade, and sometimes ironmongery and odd bits of timber too, around the streets of Birmingham. Quite often we would wave down a passing MEB vehicle which would give us a lift if space permitted. Their sudden arrival on the scene was akin to the surprise of finding an oasis when lost in a desert. Treks of this type were many and, of course, were part and parcel of the job, but some cannot be forgotten and they also give me the excuse to introduce some more of my compatriots.

Without a doubt the finest all round carpenter and joiner I ever knew was Dave. I was extremely fortunate to serve much of my apprenticeship in his care. He was the most intelligent of men, his memory was legendary and his ultimate knowledge of a whole range of subjects left those who tangled with him bemused. He was not, though, a 'know it all' for on those subjects he knew little he would remain silent. As a youngster he had easily passed exams to enter one of the King Edward grammar schools and, although a scholarship was available, his parents could not afford the school uniform. This was an obstacle which not only blighted Dave's future life but many others as well. A very deliberate barrier that ensured the working class remained in their preconceived strata of society. Thus he effectively taught himself by his unquenchable thirst for reading, non-fiction of course. He possessed the strangest of humours. The first time I met him I thought him odd. Like everyone in those days, apart from me, he smoked. On our meeting we exchanged brief 'hellos' then he suddenly turned to me;

"Nip to the shop lad and get me five wild Woodbines, I will tame them myself!"

I laughed, Dad smoked Woodbines and I had fetched them for him hundreds of times, but I hadn't heard that one before. He seemed to appreciate my laughter and he laughed too, his National Health false teeth, very ill fitting, rattled around his mouth. The start of a long and wondrous friendship.

Eighteen years earlier he had been part of Montgomery's victorious 8th army in the desert of North Africa. A turning part in the fortunes of the allies and a tremendous morale booster to the home front. He had courted death, not by the actions of the enemy, but by a ruptured stomach ulcer. He had, however, not forgotten how to trek and treated Reg's penny pinching with distain. One early such slog I remember very well, and every time that I have stumbled upon Shirley Road, Hall Green, I wince. I had arranged to meet Dave in Acocks Green. At that time Dave, appropriately, lived in Carpenters Road, Lozells and had had the foresight to leave his tools at the first of three sub-stations situated at the Acocks Green end of Shirley Road. It was, even at 8.00 am, warm and by noon had become very warm. Shirley Road then had no bus service so it was a foot slog from our first job to the other two, one in the middle and one at the far end. The actual jobs were quite small but humping tools, etc., left me close to expiring. That's when I discovered the full length of Shirley Road. Dave attempted to cheer me by saying;

"Don't worry son, there's a light at the end of the tunnel."

I must admit I couldn't see one. We finished our work on Shirley Road sub-station shortly before 1.00 pm. We continued our trek towards the 'light' promised by Dave, the M & B sign that proved to be the Robin Hood pub. Dave indicated an outside table.

"Sit there son," he said, "this is the light at the end of the tunnel."

Dave returned to the table with two pints of mild and a shandy for me. He demolished the first pint in almost one draught, the second, I could tell he savoured. Every time I see the ending of that super film Ice Cold in Alex I am reminded of that moment. Sir John Mills downing a long desired, cold beer in a bar in Alexandria, and Dave doing the same in the garden of the Robin Hood. It was ironical that Dave became one of the regulars when he left Lozells to within two hundred yards of the Robin Hood. I never asked him, but I often wondered if those two pints had influenced his decision to relocate to Hall Green.

The Department had three full time HGV drivers and one other that was loaned from the Central Garage Unit at Summer Lane, when the work load was heavy or when one of our regular drivers was on leave or off sick. Two Leyland tippers and one long flat back Bedford were the Department's complement. The drivers were real characters. It really would be very remiss of me not to recount my personal memories of them, but truly a whole tome could be devoted to the drivers of those particular transports of delight.

Bernard, Sid, Dai (Taffy) and Joe, the relief, never failed to be the source of amusement to me, although to others they caused frustration and sometimes anger. Bernard was my particular favourite. To a young lad, his tales were often fantastic and left me open-mouthed. It was of no help at all being completely unworldly, as most sixteen year olds were in those days. Sex was often on Bernard's agenda when it came to his inflated recall. On one journey to some outpost of our empire, he asked if I was still a virgin. I looked to my left where Dave sat in the passenger seat, I was sat between them, legs straddling the gear stick all very uncomfortable, there were no seat belts in those days. Dave was rattling his false teeth and relishing my obvious innocence and discomfort. Bernard changed gear;

"Ever had a girl?" he said.

I remained silent.

"I am talking about sexual intercourse," he said.

I could feel myself blushing, and I shook my head.

"It's time you got stuck in lad!" he added. "It's never too early or too late."

Dave and Bernard laughed, obviously delighting in my embarrassment. Bernard lapsed into reminiscent mood.

"You know Dave, my first time was probably one of my best. I was seduced."

We stopped at some traffic lights and Bernard lit a cigarette and inhaled deeply.

"You're a nice lad, I hope it happens to you."

As far as I know, it didn't.

But really, the love of Bernard's life was his budgerigar, Timmy. Stories of Bernard's budgie were legendary and apart from his owner's relating, unproven. One such story left me bemused for Bernard told me that Timmy could count, not just count but had mathematical reasoning that would have had Charles Darwin nonplussed. Timmy could actually count accurately the number of sacks of coal that were being delivered. In an age when few people trusted the coalman to deliver the correct amount, to Bernard, Timmy was a valuable asset. He claimed that Timmy had actually told him that he had been deprived of an cwt. bag of coal. The coalman, after some argument, had agreed and said he could have miscounted and gave Bernard another bag. This exploit made Timmy famous, in Hockley at least!

In the summer it wasn't a problem to travel on the open back of the lorry, in fact it was quite pleasant. I remember one instance though that could have turned decidedly nasty. I had opted for the back of Bernard's lorry and stood behind the cab, my arms resting on the timber 'H' section with long legs of 3" by 2" fencing timbers on either side, unsecured. Bernard drove down the old Bullring and into Digbeth and at the New Canal Street junction he had to brake violently and suddenly. The timbers flew forward with me hanging on to as many as I could. None of the timbers decamped from the vehicle, but I was left lying face down on the cab roof with my legs on the 'H' section. No-one inside the cab knew of my plight as I scrambled with timbers back to safety, before ascending the now long gone Camp Hill flyover.

Joe was the relief driver. The lenses in his spectacles were the thickness of bottle bottoms, which didn't inspire confidence in his driving abilities. The cabin space in the tipper lorries was even more cramped than Bernard's Bedford and so I found myself huddled up between various building materials as Joe navigated the city traffic on route to Hodge Hill and our work site. Extensive road works were in progress along Washwood Heath Road, effectively making this reasonably wide thoroughfare a tight two lanes. The works were on our near side and barriered for their length which must have been some five hundred yards. I sat enthralled as Joe managed to clip barrier after barrier, sending them down, like dominoes, into the excavations and onto those working in them. A chorus of Irish expletives trailed in our wake. On reaching our destination I thought it prudent to mention to Joe what had happened. He looked at me quizzically:

"What barriers son, I didn't see any barriers?" he said, shrugging his shoulders.

Sid supplemented his wages as a driver with a small income derived from tending the garden and doing odd jobs for a prominent, wealthy, local politician. Everyone liked Sid, very down to earth with a dry sense of humour. A flat cap, surmounted his well-worn features and a long navy blue mackintosh was continually in use from September to May. Nothing seemed to faze Sid. It was with some surprise though that on the untimely death of his part-time employer Sid had been left a bequest – the family car. He knew the car well for one of his duties was its care, and occasionally its driver. The Rover 95 was Sid's pride and joy. It was indeed spotless, inside and out, and its new owner was constantly polishing and attending its every whim.

The 'new' M1 had not been in operation all that long when one Saturday Sid decided to take the car for a spin to London. The Rover was travelling like a dream, both its engine and Sid purring their approval. Well into the journey he noticed in his mirror a sports car immediately behind whose driver was gesturing and flashing his headlights. Sid eventually was able to pull into a service area and the sports car drew up alongside and out stepped a well-known television and radio disc jockey.

"How much do you want for the Rover then?" he enquired.

"Sorry mate, it's not for sale," replied Sid.

The disc jockey then tested Sid's resolve with various increasing offers. The potential buyer at length decided to accept Sid's intransigence. It was at that point, that Sid realised why his treasured Rover was in such demand:

"On your money mate you could afford virtually any car you want." Sid retorted.

"It isn't the car, as nice as it is, it's the plates," the disc jockey explained.

Sid's car was blessed with the registration POP 33, he hadn't realised what a valuable asset the car possessed!

So, for the first two years of my apprenticeship mobility between jobs was either by bus and foot slog, the occasional lift and, if I was lucky, by lorry. Despite Reg's unintentional aim to see his carpenters well and truly knackered for the sake of a penny, the whole episode certainly made me physically fit and ready in the event of a third world war. It also gave me an appreciation for the fitness of my much older mentors. Of course, most of the time, we apprentices were doing the humping, a term, often used by Bernard, but in a different context and with a different aspect of pleasure.

You will, if you have been attentive, have realised that I have concluded this chapter with the omission of one character mentioned earlier – Taffy. More of him later.

7

"I Doubt It, Said The Carpenter, And Shed A Bitter Tear"
The Walrus And The Carpenter

From my Apprenticeship Indentures:

> *Sub Section (ii)*
> *The Apprentice will during the period of service:*
> *(d) Attend such courses at technical college or elsewhere as may be required by the Employers having regard to the best interests of the Apprentice.*

For the first year of my apprenticeship day release was at the internationally renowned Matthew Boulton College in the city centre.

It seemed that I had known that impressive Victorian edifice in Suffolk Street for all of my years. I knew not its purpose, to me it was just another of its architectural type in a city that bristled with such buildings. Buildings which the Luftwaffe had spared but would soon fall foul of a quirky wave of philistine architects and planners.

The Weoley Castle buses to the city terminated opposite the college in Holliday Street. They then turned into Allport Street and back into Suffolk Street, circumnavigating the West End Cinema, their first stop being outside the college on their outward journey. There had been over my previous years abundant journeys to town with mother or brother, usually on a Saturday morning, which meant, of course, that I had stood outside the college, wondering just what went on when once you had ascended those wide steps and entered its impressive portals. I was soon to find out, for I was despatched there in late August 1959 to enrol in a preliminary course, City & Guilds in Carpentry and Joinery.

I entered a building which was in the last throws of its existence and it was then that I realised the enormity and functional lavishness that encompassed the full range of building crafts therein and, of course, its multiplicity of engineering and associated trades. Matthew Boulton had a reputation nationally for producing fine craftsmen and the Building Trades department was no exception. We had excellent tutors who not only gave us students the benefit of their experience but a respect for craftsmanship, for the materials we worked with and the vast array of tools, that were then, an intricate part of our craft.

So many craftsmen owe massive debts of gratitude to those who passed on their hard earned skills and those venerable tutors at Matthew Boulton are among them. Messrs Faithorn, Richards, Crawford, Webb and many more were held in esteem by us youngsters who thrived on the enthusiasm they had for our craft. It is true that they were hard taskmasters, but so were the hard bitten craftsmen who we worked alongside on site and in workshop. Some of those were lucky enough to have enlightened employers and the chance to attend Matthew Boulton. Many others did so independently, attending evening classes in their own time after a long working day.

The tools we used in the workshop were, in many cases, quite ancient, bordering on the antique. They encompassed the finest of manufacturers, many sadly no longer in existence such as Sorby chisels, Disston and Tysack saws, Marples gauges, etc. Grateful craftsmen, ever mindful of the part the college had played in giving them a living, had bequeathed many of these tools to the college. Their names stamped on the handles of saws, chisels and wooden planes, we were indeed proud to be acquainted with them.

One rule that the college had, which was particularly unhelpful, was that of not allowing students to use the lifts. My evening class was on the very top floor of the building and concluded at 9.00 pm, no skiving off in those days, for your employer's attendance card was signed by the tutor at the end of each lesson. Unfortunately my bus left the terminus at 9.00 pm and I would race down flights of stairs from the top floor, nearly always to see my bus turning left into Navigation Street and bemoaning the half hour wait for the next one.

The 1959 preliminary year intake of apprentice carpenter and joiners were the last to be enrolled at the college. I suppose there were about twenty of us and some long standing friendships were born of that year. The following year we enrolled at the new Hall Green Technical College, a monument to all that was wrong with 60s construction and design. Completion of the college was so far behind schedule that we apprentices constructed most of the interior fittings in the department's workshops.

I am sure the more enlightened outlook of the day would have, justifiably, seen the magnificent old Matthew Boulton College spared, or at least its wonderful façade, for we would realise now it truly was irreplaceable. Its value in terms of producing a skilled and renowned work force for our city and nation cannot be calculated.

It was, however, an integral element in the vibrancy of a city whose basis of prosperity was in the entrepreneurial nuance of the pioneers of the industrial revolution and, perhaps more importantly, craftsmen with fine skills that complemented such endeavour and futuristic thinking.

8

"Old Soldiers Never Die, They Just Fade Away"

In many ways one of the highlights of the day was the lunchtime break which was officially for thirty minutes, but often went on for up to an hour in work situations away from our Piers Road Depot. This was especially so when other trades would share our breaks with us. The discussion and banter ranged from the highly humorous to the wholly serious and covered an extremely broad spectrum. Sport, of course, featured prominently. Football, cricket, horse and dog racing, boxing and even, I remember of one occasion, the boat race. Politics and religion were the catalysts for some very heated debates, often never resolved and carried over to another day when the participants met again. For me all very fascinating, although any contributions I may have had to give would have been treated with distain, if I had dared to intercede.

In 1959 the Second World War was still a very recent memory. The Department had a cross section of ex-service men; some had served in both World Wars, most in one or the other. It was often the topic of discussion at lunchtime. The memories of old soldiers. Those memories were as diverse as the moods and emotions they created. Some such as Horace, who had survived the western front with the Lancashire Fusiliers remained silent and searched for distraction in the pages of a newspaper. Often the subject was quickly dropped, for those who had served in the second conflict had difficulty in comprehending the sacrifice Horace and their fathers had given in the war to end all wars! Working with Horace, who then was in his late 60s, was always a pleasure for when he was deeply engrossed in his work he lapsed into a range of First World War melodies, some of which had clever, and not very edifying, adaptions to the original lyrics.

What was a factor though, was that most of the stories about service life were hilarious. I suspect some had been slightly exaggerated for a basis of fact. Each story seemed to generate more from other sources and the inter-service rivalry was intense.

Fred was a scaffolder, one of the best I knew. He had served in an infantry regiment in the second war. Having got drunk in a North African bar, he had woken in a brothel, with a comrade who was also in a very fragile state. They rushed back to camp to find the invasion of Sicily was underway and they had missed their allotted boat. They were given a dressing down, which Fred admitted would have been a worse punishment but for the turmoil at that particular time. He and his comrade were packed off to Sicily. Further punishment was exacted on him as his unit were in the forefront of the Italian campaign which he said, seemed never ending.

Harry was even older than Horace and had been a scaffolder in the days of poles and lashings (timber and rope). He already had long service and, as with most of the older ones, had originally been employed by the city's Electricity Supply Department. His scaffolding days had long since ended, and he now eased through what remained of his working days as a general labourer and would often drift off in a little world of his own. He was short and stocky with glasses which always seemed set at the end of his nose and he wore a very large checked flat cap. Harry was not known for his generosity, and was not easy to find, especially when a collection was in the offing. His downfall, however, were the fumes and smoke emitted from the filling of Navy Shag which seemed permanently in his pipe. My first meeting with Harry was one summer's morning. Reg had collared me from my onerous duties in the Joiners Shop to assist one of my mentors at a sub-station in Streetley, a destination I knew nothing of but had seen while waiting for a Midland Red at the central bus station in town. Having checked my financial resources Reg issued me with plastic tokens for my journey to the terminus of the Kingstanding corporation bus.

"You can walk the rest of the way, don't bother with the red bus, it's only a couple of stops."

I never thought I would reach my destination and my mentor was surprised at my arrival, knackered.

"You have not walked from the terminus of the Kingstanding bus, son?"

I nodded. The bricklayer and his mate sniggered, and Harry puffed on his pipe. My mate made the assumption that perhaps Reg's parents had not entered into wedlock!

Later in the afternoon Harry asked where I lived. Before I had time to answer, my mate said:

"Harry, you could give the lad a lift."

"Weoley Castle," I said.

"Give us a couple of bob and I'll drop you at Selly Oak, I live in Stirchley." Harry replied.

Harry had a car; it was parked outside the sub-station, an absolutely immaculate Austin Ruby, highly polished and pristine. At 5.30 pm Harry and I bade goodnight to the others and walked over to the Austin Ruby.

"Hang on a bit," said Harry.

He opened the driver's door and from the seat picked up a starting handle, two swings and the Ruby spluttered into life. I went to open the passenger door.

He bent down into the passenger well and rolled back a piece of carpet, revealing a missing floor board.

"You will have to put your feet on either side of the hole," he said. "Don't look down at the road; I don't want you being sick!"

We eventually commenced our journey, turning onto the main Chester Road. Harry drove with complete concentration, I thought. His nose and spectacles no more than three inches from the windscreen, his cap pulled down and clutching the steering wheel in a vice like grip, gazing through a fog of tobacco smoke. We fairly rattled down the Chester Road at a maximum speed of 25 mph, towards the busy junction and traffic lights at Bakers Lane. We were some 200 yards away when the lights went against us. Harry kept going, closer and closer – my hand reached for the leather handle and my feet pressed hard into the floor. I leaned back in anticipation of the inevitable crash but fate favoured the Ruby and its occupants. I looked across at the driver and wondered just where he was, for he certainly wasn't on the Chester Road. I was very pleased to disembark at the junction of Bristol Road and Heeley Road, Selly Oak. Harry finally spoke:

"You will have to take the bus tomorrow morning, I like being early and I don't know how reliable you are."

"Thanks Harry," I said. "I think that's probably best."

That was my first and last ride in the Ruby, but I must ask if a young lad's life is worth just 2s.

However, I digress. Harry had served in both world wars. He rarely spoke of either and I assumed that his First World

War experience had been, like so many young men of his generation, a very painful period of his life. In the second conflict Harry had spent the war in a Territorial Army Royal Artillery 'Backpack' unit, based at Hams Hall power station on the edge of the city near Coleshill. The huge cooling towers of Hams Hall and Nechells power stations were prominent navigational points for enemy bombers approaching the city from the East. Ostensively the unit was situated there to protect the power station and it was made up mainly of Electricity Supply workers.

There was, however, an event which happened during Harry's service with that unit which generated much amusement, anger in some quarters, and embarrassment to those involved including Harry. When he was around the subject was never mentioned and indeed if any indication that conversation may be swaying towards the hostilities, Harry would quietly puff away out of earshot. Not difficult for he spent much time cupping his hand around his right ear in an attempt to improve his reception.

Legend has it that Harry and company may have imbibed at a local hostelry before manning their posts at Hams Hall, which could have prompted the knee jerk reaction which later occurred. Suddenly, in the skies above them, appeared a lone fighter heading in their direction. The unit quickly sprang into action and opened fire, the fighter quickly banked away and made off. It was at this point that the 'spotter' realised his error, for clearly the aircraft was one of ours – a Spitfire! The proverbial hit the fan and it was not long before a staff car appeared and the unit faced very irate top brass. They were, of course, very severely censured.

The implications for the war effort and fighter production in particular, could have in all truth, been compromised, for the fighter had just come off the production line and it had the legendary Alex Henshaw at the controls. The test pilot, stationed at nearby Castle Bromwich, many years later in an interview gave the story authenticity. Thus in this aspect Harry and his unit had achieved a status of notoriety and celebrity that no other ex-servicemen would want!

I always felt sorry, during these lunchtime sessions, for those who had been debarred military service because they were in a building trade. One such was Bob, a really nice bloke and a good carpenter, who hailed from Nottinghamshire. He had tried desperately to join the RAF. Near his home were a number of RAF stations and he had worked at some of them for a local builder. The Blitz had just started and Bob was quickly utilized repairing bomb damage in Birmingham and Coventry. He was never released from this chore for the duration of the war and had to forego his military experience. The war ended, Bob had met his future wife and the impetus had gone.

One story however, that the frustrated Bob told, always evoked much laughter and sympathy. Eventually, as happened quite often at that time, his mother-in-law became infirm and moved in with Bob, his wife and children. Unfortunately Bob and his mother-in-law just did not get on which caused a great deal of friction in his little terraced house. So much so that any chance of overtime offered was quickly snaffled by the much put upon Bob.

Eventually Bob, one of the two carpenters who could drive, acquired a second hand and elderly Morris Minor which he was forever tinkering with to keep it road worthy. He hated Sundays for his wife insisted that, whatever the weather, they go for a 'little run' in the Morris. The little run always reached its climax in Henley-in-Arden where they stopped for one of its renowned ice creams. Due to her suspect legs, mother-in-law always adorned the passenger seat with Bob's wife in the back. The ice creams would be eaten and the trio would make for home. The route took them past Yardley parish church where Bob and his wife had married many years earlier. Every Sunday as they passed the beautiful old church, the slightly demented mother-in-law, would turn to Bob and say:

"One of my daughter's was married there!"
Bob's reply was always unrepeatable and under his breath.

After many such Sunday excursions, and being completely fed up with the same words of observation, words which Bob would mouth into the rear view mirror for the benefit of his wife before reaching the landmark, he decided enough was enough and changed route to bypass the church. They arrived home in silence and Bob and his wife got out of the car. Mother-in-law remained seated and made no move to disembark. Bob opened the passenger door:

"We're home ma," he said.

"No we ain't," said mother-in-law. "We haven't passed the church."

"Come on, ma," Bob pleaded. "We've come back another way."

"But I wanted to go the other way, past the church."

"Now why is that?" asked Bob.

"Well, one of my daughters got married there," was the reply. So, to keep the peace and to get mother-in-law out of the car Bob had to drive back to Yardley and go past the church. He never took a detour again.

As mentioned in a previous chapter, Dave had seen nearly all his war service in North Africa with the Royal Ordinance Corps. He had been in a military hospital in Egypt for a period of time, having been operated on for a ruptured stomach ulcer, I once saw the scars and they were enormous. Every few hours an orderly would bring his medication which was dispensed from a HP Sauce bottle. Every time he saw the bottle his mind would drift to Aston Cross, just a short distance from his home. One day, the hospital had a visit from top brass, headed by Field Marshal Montgomery himself. Monty gave a cursory glance at Dave, whose torso was swathed in bandage and probably in a more parlous state than some of those in the hospital who had survived a close encounter with the enemy.

In the next bed to Dave was a young Irish private from an infantry regiment who had sustained a bullet wound and to whom Dave had become quite friendly, the lad's surname was Rehar. As the group passed through the ward the more junior officers would stop and chat to the patients. One of them suddenly stopped at the young private's bed.

"Private Rehar," he said. "Good job you weren't in the artillery." He laughed and moved on.

"Pratt!" said Dave. (The equivalent rank of private in the artillery was gunner!)

The officer heard and glanced across at Dave; he saw what was obviously a seriously ill soldier and decided against taking any further action.

"Don't take any notice son; he has probably never fired a shot in anger." Dave said to his fellow patient.

Dennis was the other charge-hand carpenter and joiner. His main duty was to oversee the maintenance and well-being of the Birmingham Area Offices in Dale End and Fazeley Street. He was also in charge of the construction and setting up of exhibition stands at Bingley Hall and other venues for the various trades' shows which took place during the year.

Dennis had built a little empire for himself which was quite often at odds with his foreman. Reg was well into his 60s; Dennis when I first met him was just 34. Having set his domain in a location where he made himself an indispensable asset, he was then at the service and patronised by the upper echelons of management. As such, Dennis was never seen in overalls or apron, but in a crisp brown cow-gown, which made the statement 'I'm in charge' and he was. More of that later.

Dennis had eventually been called up for military service as the war had just ended. He had been posted to Northern Ireland, and it was there that he met his future wife who lived in Londonderry. His army service had been 'almost a waste of time', but on demob he returned to Birmingham and married, resuming his job in the now nationalised industry. His dominancy at work however, did not extend to his home life, for there was absolutely no doubt as to who was in charge there. Indeed his wife would often tell whoever was around to hear that very fact. We were all of the opinion that if he could, Dennis would sever all links with his Londonderry in-laws, as he became more and more involved in the nasty situation developing in that country.

Dennis' wife and her family were not only passionate about, but were deeply committed, to the Orange Order. Unfortunately for Dennis, who would do anything for a quiet life, he was also expected now to share his wife's and in-laws' commitment to all things Orange. To this end and no doubt under some pressure, and probably a little worse for wear, he had sworn allegiance to the cause when visiting his in-laws on a holiday. He probably thought that would be the apex of his involvement, but his wife had other ideas.

Dennis was never early for work and never late either. He would time his entrance to the carpenters shop, in the Dale

End complex, between 7.45 and 7.55 am. Knowing this routine I was already on my feet to pour him and sometimes his wife, who worked in the city, a fresh cup of tea. On this particular morning he had arrived on his own, his greeting was shallow as he changed into his cow-gown and flopped into his revolving chair. He stared gloomily at the ceiling as I placed his cup of tea before him. I gave a quick glance to Dave who shrugged his shoulders. At 8.00 am Dave rose from his chair and I picked up the now empty cups.

"I don't suppose you know anyone who I could loan a bowler hat from?" enquired Dennis suddenly.

Sensing that Dennis was not ready for work, Dave sat down again.

"I think we will have another cuppa," said Dennis.

I quickly washed the cups and made three more teas. I remained on my feet, not wanting to push my luck during this very unexpected occurrence.

"Tell me you aren't going to do it," said Dave.

Dennis looked at Dave quizzically.

"Do what," said Dennis.

"Go on an Orange parade," added Dave.

"How the hell did you know?"

"I can't think of any other reason why you would want a bowler hat," answered Dave.

"I don't want to, but she insists," returned Dennis.

"My dad's got a bowler hat, it belonged to my granddad, I'm sure you could borrow it," I said.

Dennis' intention to parade around Londonderry soon became common knowledge, it provoked a range of comments, but no-one could foresee its effect on some members of the department's staff. Despite an unfortunate air of superiority, Dennis was easy to get on with, he knew his job and was a good organiser and generally well liked by the staff. However we had, particularly among the large contingent of painters and decorators, a high proportion of Irish Catholics although none from Ulster. When Dennis' intentions became known, a sudden chill wind ensued from that quarter.

Liverpool Jim from the Everton faction of the city shook his head:

"Dennis won't do it more than once," he observed.

Dennis tried on the bowler, it was far too small. If skull size equates to stature its ill-fitting should have been predictable, Granddad Betteridge was 5' 4", and Dennis on the other hand was 6' 3".

"It will do," said Dennis.

The bowler sat like a pimple on Dennis' head. Jim expressed the opinion that one of the lads would be taking a pot-shot at it, and I feared for the bowler's wellbeing. The Orange march came and went and the bowler was returned undamaged. Dennis never said a word and no-one asked but it was his first and last Orange march! The clouds were forming over the province which heralded a bloody and tragic chapter in the country's history. On reflection Dennis, as an outsider, was perhaps more perceptive to that change. I wondered if he rued, as time passed, his service posting to the province.

Liverpool Jim's war service had affected him deeply, what he saw he would rarely elaborate on. However, we did once talk at length about his war. Like Fred, earlier in this chapter, Jim had fought his way from Sicily almost the length of Italy. The war for Jim was a life-changing and challenging experience. He had been a child of the great depression, which blighted the years between the two world wars. One of a large family, he had spent his early years in a terrace house in the maze of streets in Liverpool's dockland.

The deprivation of those years, however, had not prepared Jim for Naples for there he witnessed real poverty. The wizen faces of young children, begging in the streets, and forced into prostitution for the gratification of invading armies was a lasting memory for him. Naples, a sea port, was perhaps too much of a likeness to Liverpool for Jim, whose own experiences in his early life, had an affinity but not the severity of those who suffered in its ruins.

His salvation was his faith. A realisation that if he were devout enough, and dedicated enough, perhaps he could make a difference in helping those in need. Naples held him in a vice like grip, constantly returning to haunt him and giving him pointers as to where his life should progress. None of us questioned Jim's faith, he had faith in abundance but that faith would be balanced with the desire to enjoy life as much as possible, and he did. He once told me that he had considered entering a monastery but the vow of celibacy was perhaps a step too far, and he felt he would be of more use doing good works at grass roots. His holidays were spent assisting the seriously ill and the desperate to visit Lourdes. Every Sunday he would assist a priest at mass in signing his words for the profoundly deaf. Jim had taught himself to sign when he discovered that there was a desperate need for such a service.

Jim was a wonderful ballroom dancer and any social event would see him constantly in demand by females of all ages, shapes and sizes. For Jim could make even the most moderate of partners look and feel like Ginger Rogers. He would be almost permanently on his feet, returning fleetingly to base to refuel – a pint of mild and a tot of whisky. We would sit in wonder at his 'pulling power' and realised his reluctance to take Holy Orders. Quite often, in quiet moments, when he thought no-one was around he would lapse into practise, a quickstep, waltz or foxtrot, throwing in the odd fish-tail and chasse, and having obvious delight at his own proficiency, his highly polished brown brogues shining in a whirl of terpsichorean footwork.

Dave, who had no abilities at all when it came to dancing, did, however, have a theory as to Jim's popularity as a dance partner. At one event he had been watching Jim closely, gliding across the floor with a succession of partners, who had literally made a grab for him when his refuelling had ceased.

"Got it," exclaimed Dave. "Look where his right leg is, no wonder they are queuing up for him!"

Easter bank holidays always troubled Jim. He felt everyone who had even a semblance of Christian belief should not work on Good Friday. He could never quite get to grip with the concept of a Monday, Tuesday Easter holiday as practiced in the West Midlands. True to his convictions Jim would always reserve one day's holiday to take on Good Friday.

To Jim, Christmas was just as important, not for just its religious meaning, but also for his personal pilgrimage to Liverpool to visit his family. Christmas Eve would see him board the train at New Street Station bound for Liverpool's Lime Street. One such journey, however, did cause great anxiety to us all, for the train he was travelling on was derailed after a collision. There were fatalities, many injured and no trace at all of Jim. On the 28th December, he walked into the carpenters shop as if nothing had happened. Jim's railway carriage had been unscathed; he had helped out at the scene and then continued onto Liverpool. I don't think any incident would curtail his Christmas visit to his kin folk.

Jim had no fear of death and looked forward to an extension of his charitable works in his retirement. Sadly after a short illness he died the day after his 65th birthday, a loss to all and especially to those who depended on him so much. What direction would his life have taken if his war had been different?

I spent a fair proportion of my early apprenticeship under the tutorage of Horace. He had what should have been a major disability for someone whose hands were perhaps the most important factor in his craft. I always thought that he had lost two fingers of his right hand in an accident with a woodworking machine, a common occurrence with woodworkers when machines were less reliable. However, during one lunch break he told me that his fingers had been lost during his service in the First World War with the Lancashire Fusiliers on the Western Front at the Battle of Arras. A bullet from an enemy rifle had hit the barrel of his own weapon and travelled down the stock of his rifle to his hand.

For Horace, being right handed, it was a terrible handicap when he returned to Civvy Street and wanted to continue in the craft for which he had trained. A hire and fire system awaited any building worker in the twenties and thirties and Horace explained that he quickly had to become ambidextrous with a wife and young family to support. He was, however, an exceedingly proficient craftsman.

It was my pleasure, albeit sometimes a painful one, to be taught by Horace and the other old hands, all of whom had his wealth of knowledge and experience. They all had a vast vocabulary of building trade jargon that, to a lad straight from secondary school, sounded an alien tongue. Such sayings as 'cods head' – a protruding nail, 'wart' – a raised knot and 'half-crown' – and indentation caused by a hammer head in timber, and there were many others commonly used.

Horace lived in Cotteridge and worked many times for the legendary builder, Mick Grant, whose deeds he would spend many an Outer-Circle bus journey home, recalling with enthusiasm. Horace was a character who had the most flamboyant of entrances into the Joiners Shop in the morning. From the entrance door, and from a distance of about 15 feet, he was able to home his much loved and battered trilby onto his allocated hat and coat peg with ease. Many an unsuspecting newcomer would find himself out of pocket in doubting Horace's ability to perform this feat. I was, of course, not able to risk any part of my £2. 4s weekly wage! Always generous, he would often sense when I was a bit short of money and pay my bus fare from Handsworth to Selly Oak. It really is amazing to me how that generation of workers retained a sense of fun and fair play after the way society had treated them for so long.

Horace, of course, is long since gone bless his soul, but long after his retirement some of us were still trying to perform his hat trick – with little success! We concluded that the answer lay in a certain well-worn brown trilby and a three digit throwing hand.

More of Horace in a later chapter.

9

And In Remembrance

In the Accounts Section of Birmingham Area Offices in Dale End, which was where many people paid their electricity bills, was a very fitting tribute to workers of the City of Birmingham's Electricity Supply Department who gave their lives in the First World War.

The cast bronze plaque, bearing a beautifully enamelled city coat of arms, carries the names of thirty-one men, the majority of whom served in the county regiment, the Royal Warwickshires. Every November a wreath of poppies was placed at its location, a tribute which continued into the early 1960s. Although at the time I never enquired if any of the men I worked with, and had served in that war, knew those commemorated on the memorial but it is entirely possible.

Unfortunately the recognition of their sacrifice lapsed but was revived in 2003 when the memorial was rescued and is now proudly on display in the city council house where other such memorials are located. The memorial is now protected as all known war memorials are by a parliamentary act.

10

"No Man Should Return Home Tired From His Labours"

According to Liverpool Jim the words of a Pope, but he could never remember which one!

Liverpool Jim would often quote these lines at the end of a particularly tiresome day. Dave, whose roots were in 19th century German Judaism, reckoned that it was more about leaving sufficient energy to procreate the Catholic faith. It was a theory that Jim agreed could be entirely possible.

In the 60s in Birmingham a film was made which, incidentally stared an icon of that era Cilla Black, and was entitled Work is a Four Letter Word. I never did see the film and I was well into my apprenticeship when it was made but the title did fascinate me. Often on the journey home, on the top deck of a No. 22 bus, tired and for the want of better things to do, I would try and substitute words in the title with other applicable four letter variations. Those words reflected my demeanour or the working day I had endured. There are plenty of permutations, but I would nearly always prefix 'work' with 'hard'.

So this chapter is all about not just work but individual jobs that will be forever with me, but need to be recorded for posterity before age befuddles the memory, for there are few others now who could recall them. New characters will be introduced.

THE VERY FIRST JOB

I suppose it was around noon on my second day, my head still spinning from trying to fully digest the many and seemingly endless duties I was expected to perform. My fellow apprentice and mentor, Ray, who had been an absolute gem, had been despatched from the Joiners Shop to site and I was on my own. I was just deliberating Ray's list of duties when I heard Bert call my name, and turned to see him standing beside lengths of deep brown coloured timber which had just been brought up from the Mill.

The timber had been planed and now, Bert told me, it had to be cleaned up for French Polishing. I didn't have a clue what to do but Bert gave me instruction in the use of a cabinet scraper and how to correctly fold and use glass paper. It looked easy, but the use of the cabinet scraper was extremely arduous. The timber that not even the machinists knew the name of, and they were real experts in timber identification, was bought as a job lot during the timber rationing years. It was probably from West Africa and was extremely hard and uncompromising, truly awful to machine; its use was the prelude to sharpening saws, planer and any other machine that had the misfortune to come into contact with the mystery wood. It was, of course, the same scenario for hand tools also, and there was no love lost between timber and Joiner. When all the hard work was complete, however, and final finish of French polish applied, it was magnificent.

My first job was also the last of the mystery timber. Its wonderful individuality could be seen in shops, showrooms and conference rooms across the Birmingham area on counters, shop and office fittings. Scraping this timber was a job any Joiner would try and shirk, Bert all but admitted that fact but he obviously thought it a befitting baptism for a lad straight from school.

For those who have never come across the afore-mentioned scraper, it is a piece of pliable steel, about 1/16th of an inch in thickness and approximately 6" x 3" in size. As the scraper is pushed along with the grain of the timber, pressure is applied by the thumbs of both hands to the centre of the tool which enables the cutting edge of the scraper to act as a very fine plane to remove any discrepancies and, eventually, produce a sleek and shiny surface. Bert, of course, did not mention the friction burns that soon developed on the soft thumbs as heat developed twixt timber and metal. The burns then turned to blisters on the balls of each thumb. Bert told me to dip them in cold water every now and then. This brought some relief but I am sure I could hear a sizzling sound as cold water came into contact with hot tortured skin. I was advised not to plaster them as it would make them worse and they were bound in rags, for ease of working the blisters were punctured with the corner of a sharp chisel. My thumbs were that sore by the third day I had difficulty removing coins from my pocket for my bus fare. I dare not have shown my mother for she would have demanded an end to such cruelty but by the fifth day my thumbs were oblivious to pain and the mild infection that had set in, but never had a chance to develop.

I had, I hoped, reached the end of my first job and only Bert and Bill's critical inspection remained. They had to work with what I had prepared for them and at my bidding Bert limped his way to the two benches that I, and my tormentors, occupied. He carefully inspected each length, looking along the grain and his caressing hands moved across the timber to each flaw to which so much of my time and pain had been devoted.

"Not bad lad, not bad at all," he said. "A few bits here and there, but they will probably cut out. Not bad lad, not bad at all," he repeated.

So that was it, and I soon knew that any praise had to be earned, often in a hard and painful way.

A few weeks later I saw what Bert and Bill had achieved with my preparatory work and I felt pride that I had played my part. In the Joiners Shop stood a counter and shop fitting of beautiful proportions and wonderful curvature.

"What do you think of them lad?"

"They are wonderful Bert," I said.

"You played your part lad, and I hope now it has been worthwhile."

I could not deny that it truly had, despite the blisters.

11

"Don't You Know What They Are Son?"

I suppose I was a few weeks into my apprenticeship and finding it hard going, but strangely very satisfying. A fact which, if I had time to spare, I probably would have contemplated more deeply but the Joiners Shop clock had finally got to 8.00 am.

Like those sophisticated time pieces in town squares and on important buildings, a door opens and the character, or several, proclaim the hour. The door to the Joiners workshop would open and Reg would herald his appearance with a 'morning all', timed to perfection. As a result of this reoccurring phenomenon, newspapers were stowed away and teacups emptied, overalls and aprons donned and tools ready by 7.59 and 59 seconds. I soon learned that Reg's demeanour could be determined by the inflection in his greeting. I came not to expect any conversation from Reg directed at me, only to ask briefly my wellbeing. This morning, however, was different. He stopped at the huge lead sink where I was washing emptied mugs and cups (yes, I did say lead!).

"Get yourself ready by 12.15 lad, you're coming out with me and you won't be back for a bit." I had no time to ask where. The door was closing on the clock and he had to re-enter the workings! I stood for a moment, a bit bemused, and glanced over to old Horace, who occupied the bench nearest to the sink.

"Don't worry son, you are going to work at head office in Dale End. You'll be there a few weeks with lots of nice girls." He looked over his spectacles and smiled.

Reg entered the workshop on the dot to collect me. I bade my 'goodbyes' and followed Reg to the parking area where the backdoors of a small van were open for me to get inside, our lift to Dale End was to be courtesy of the foreman painter. The back of the van was packed with tins of paint, dust sheets, packs of brushes and sandpaper. It was a short but uncomfortable journey. I alighted at the Moor Street entrance to the offices smelling of turps and tending an attack of cramp. I knew that if I had to keep up with Reg I would need to be 100% fit. Reg was in top form and I struggled to keep in touch through offices, along corridors, up and down flights of stairs. A succession of doors, double and single, seemed always about to close as I approached with a rear view of my foreman's profile heading rapidly to the next opening. His progress had the continual accompaniment of, 'Morning Reg' and 'Alright Reg, how you going our kid?' and other such offerings of greetings. It seemed that everyone knew Reg, but he confined himself to 'Morning' for everyone.

Eventually, and thankfully, we finally arrived at the Carpenters Shop as I was wondering just how I was going to find my way around a building which gave every indication of an enigma of Hampton Court maze proportions.

The Carpenters Shop had three occupants, two in brown overalls with the almost compulsory flat caps, and one with a brown cow-gown. The cow-gown was, of course, the aforementioned Dennis, one of the overall wearers was Dave, my first meeting, and the stocky little Welshman known as Ben. The three were engrossed; studying a large architect's drawing which was spread across the largest of Joiner's

69

benches. Reg entered with his usual cheery 'morning' which was acknowledged by the others. He then introduced me and almost immediately pointed to the kettle and tray, with its motley assortment of cups and mugs.

"Tea, lad," he said and joined the others pouring over the drawings.

I found my way around the tea making procedure in my new location and presented my four mentors with tea at the workbench and awaited further instruction.

"Come and have a look son," said Dave. "This is what you will be working on."

The drawing was amazing and almost incomprehensible to me. It was an exhibition stand which would eventually take pride of place at the Ideal Homes exhibition at Bingley Hall. The stand was to be built, sectionalised, in a former YMCA gymnasium, the buildings of which were now incorporated within the MEB range of offices and workshops in Dale End. As I was very quickly to discover, however, the exhibition stand had to be built in conjunction with a very wide variation of general repairs and maintenance associated with an extremely large and complex building.

Ben was a really nice bloke, in the same mould as Dave, very knowledgeable and a good tradesman who didn't suffer fools easily. I would happily have served the whole of my apprentice-ship with Ben, Dave and Bert for I am sure that if Ben had stayed longer with us he would have had as much influence on my training as the other two. He was a real live wire, always on the go, and expecting everyone else with whom he worked to be the same, and that suited me fine. Ben was no more than 5' 2", and Dave reckoned he needed a pair of steps to fit a skirting board! He was, however, an extremely unhealthy build and almost perpetually perspiring. In those days no-one would recognize the symptoms of a heart attack waiting to happen or very high blood pressure. Ben was only with us for eighteen months and then, to my chagrin, he left for purely financial reasons for our pay was deplorable at that time and Ben had a large family to feed. I often wonder what happened to him.

One day I called him Benjamin. He quickly told me to stick to 'Ben' for Benjamin was not his name. Sometime later I visited my great uncle who lived in Brecon and had worked all his life in the mines of the South Wales valleys. He took me to see those grey, austere villages which were not enhanced by a depressing drizzle that day. The slated roofs glistened but nothing else could lighten the grey apparel that encapsulated every building and seemingly every person who dwelt there. Then there it was on a street corner, an unobtrusive typically Welsh Victorian singular building with a low, wrought iron fence on its boundary walls, the gothic inscription above the door proclaiming the 'Ebenezer Chapel 1880'. So that was it, Ben's Christian name I bet.

On my return to work I could not wait to be working with my Welsh mentor and to have the opportunity to test my theory. The moment soon came when I was to ask 'Ebenezer' if he was ready for his afternoon cuppa. His head shot up from his work:

"How did you find out boy?" he said.

I told him of my travels in the mining villages of South Wales and he laughed.

"No boy," he said. "You know and I know, and if anybody else calls me Ebenezer I'll know where it came from!"

From then on the subject was never broached again and Ben was forever Ben.

One morning Dennis, Ben and I were having our morning break when the Carpenters Shop telephone rang, Dennis took the call and even I could hear the frantic pleas of the caller. Dennis was never fazed and was so laid back it was amazing he remained vertical. The call ended and Dennis drained the remains of his bone china cup, contemplated for a moment and then said:

"Come on lads, let's go and see what all the panic is."

Dennis picked up two sets of drain rods, Ben three pairs of wellington boots and I was despatched to the house foreman for two gallons of disinfectant. We met in the cart way to the Moor Street entrance of the building. A large manhole cover set in the cart way was lifting and dropping back into position as liquid sewage oozed out and onto the surrounding area. The stench was appalling and the admin officer was retching over a drain in the corner of the car park, one hand supporting himself on an adjacent wall. Dennis shrugged his shoulders and nudged Ben, their faces wreathed in smiles. They pulled on the wellington boots and I followed suit. Dennis produced three lifting keys for the manhole cover and gave me one of them. Normally four would have been required but the cover was bubbling away from the pressure from below. Using this factor to advantage the cover lifted quite easily. Dennis had warned me to jump clear on the cover removal and I was exceedingly pleased I did, for the sewage burst forth with the ferocity of a tsunami as at least some of the pressure from numerous blocked toilets was eased. We peered into the manhole:

"Where's all that cotton wool come from?" I said.

Ben and Dennis looked at me quizzically.

"Don't you know what they are?" said Ben.

I shook my head.

"Got any sisters?" asked Ben.

I shook my head again.

"Those lad," said Dennis, "are the plumbers nightmare, sanitary towels, and despite numerous notices they still keep flushing them down the toilets."

Dennis was not amused and conveyed his feelings forcibly to a pale and queasy admin officer, who promised to sort it out with the female staff. It says much for the innocence of youth and lack of sex education at the time, but I hadn't a clue what my mentors were talking about.

The drain rods were coupled together and Dennis attached a large screw fitting on the business end.

"Wait for the bang lad and watch that lot go," he said.

He and Ben skilfully found the manhole's outlet and fed in the rods, turning them at the same time. The rods were then slowly drawn back and a loud whoosh followed and the manhole and drain run emptied immediately. We doused ourselves and our equipment in disinfectant, our work done, the cleaning up under the instruction of Dennis, done by two labourers using gallons of disinfectant and water. Quite an experience in many ways and a far cry from carpentry and joinery but, not from building maintenance, and that was for me an invaluable lesson. At least it left me determined to find out exactly what Dennis and Ben were talking about when they were looking down that manhole!

12

Oh, Oh Antonio, He's Gone Away

*Old Music Hall song, much loved by
my mother and grandmother.*

Dale End could be quite a lonely place for the appointed apprentice when no major works were being undertaken and just Dennis, and maybe another carpenter, dealt with the routine maintenance there and at Island House, Fazeley Street.

The carpenters shop was tucked away and it is doubtful if the majority of people who worked in the complex would have any idea of its existence. They did, however, know that there were a permanent complement of carpenters and joiners for work was plentiful and very varied. Hardly an hour passed without the ring of the internal telephone informing us of some problem or minor panic. Dennis, of course, was the perfect foil for the panic stricken. Rolling his eyes, nodding occasionally, and lounging even lower in his swivel chair. The longer the caller persisted in pressing the urgency of the work, the greater the chance that Dennis would cover the mouthpiece of the phone with his free hand and whisper; "Tea lad!"

So it was always pleasant to have the company of other elements of the Building Department, the occasional brickie and mate, a passing painter or maybe a contractor's plumbers. All of course were made welcome, provided they contributed to the Tea Fund. Tony was a labourer who would be required to assist from time to time. Tony, or Antonio to give him his correct name, was a former Italian prisoner of war who had stayed in Britain at the end of the conflict. He had married and had several children and had the looks of a matinee idol and could charm the birds from a tree. The ladies adored him and as such he loved Dale End, for within its walls were an abundance of the 'fairer sex'. There was jealousy, animosity and envy from those who saw Tony as a threat and hindrance to their own prowess with the ladies. Truth to say no male had a chance when he was around. When he would eventually finish his stint at Dale End we were continually badgered by a never ending stream of women who had fallen head over heels for 'bloody Casanova' as Dave would call him. It was left to us to fend off requests for his address, where he was working, was he married and personal details which we could not answer anyhow.

"Sure as day and night he will put one of them in the club one of these days," said Liverpool Jim. Because of his war service in Italy and strong links to Catholicism, it was decided that he should have a word with him, reminding him of his marital status and his 'bambinos'. Jim could speak a Scouse version of Neapolitan Italian, which would often herald an expression of extreme incomprehension from Tony. We all thought, however, that it would be a nice personal touch despite Tony's English being far better than Jim's mangling of the Italian language. Whether Tony understood the gist of what Jim was trying to put across I don't know but it had no affect for he was just a magnet for the fairer sex. Tony's downfall was his lack of motivation for what he was actually paid for – work! As Dave remarked his only motivation was between his legs. Although we all got on with Tony it was only the constant urging and telling him what to do that would keep him at his task. His eyes were invariably elsewhere!

There is only so much one can do to cover a basic urge to idle and his lack of urgency began to be noticed by the Deputy Building Superintendent, Harry Maroney. He was a waspish character with a broad Lancashire accent and time only for those who 'put in their hours'. He didn't suffer fools or being taken for a fool and, but for the restraining hand of Department Head, Jim Slade, our turnover of staff would have been substantial. I am pleased to say he respected good tradesmen and had a soft spot for apprentices; provided you remembered his four spoons of sugar in his strong tea, which had to be in a china cup not a mug. This was unusual for someone who had spent his working life in the building trade. It became apparent to everyone, except the amorous Tony, that Mr. Maroney was taking more than an interest in him and his activities. Due warning was unheeded and it was but a short time before Harry would draw Tony, like a spider, into his web and therefore engineer his demise.

Tony had taken an age to do a fairly routine task, one that was far from onerous, when an unexpected visit from Harry caught Tony off guard, not difficult to do, and the boss had seen enough. Even all those years ago a sacking at MEB was not something achieved easily and Harry wanted to be certain of 'landing his fish'. Tony was extremely vain and, although his tasks were often demeaning, it was his job. However, he came and went from work looking immaculate which in no way reflected his sometimes mucky and menial work. So when Harry requested that Tony finish his task at Dale End and take a pickaxe, shovel and fork from Dale End across the city to Henrietta Street he got the expected reaction from Tony. In front of Dennis, Dave and me Tony adamantly refused.

"I a knowa takea de picka, shovela and a forka upa Dale End and a Bulla Street and de Arcada downa Snowa Hill to de Henrietta Street. No I don't."

Tony stood with hands on hips, Harry knew exactly what he was doing, and we knew to. Refusal to carry out a reasonable order was dismissal. Harry told him that he was sacked and to report to Piers Road. Tony departed with a two fingered gesture and, according to Jim, the equivalent of a well-known expletive in Italian. That was the last anyone saw of Tony. There could have been a mass walk out of female staff from Dale End at that very instant.

The novelty of the amorous Italian wore off eventually, although there were still enquiries and I suspect a few damp handkerchiefs when we related that he wouldn't be coming back to Dale End. Over the next months when we heard of another expectant member of staff well – we did wonder! Tony was with us but a short time, but he certainly made some impact.

13

This Request Is For ...

The former YMCA buildings in Dale End possessed a truly beautiful terracotta façade which, removed of its grime, would have surely been preserved in more enlightened times. Indeed the whole building had an element of class for an entity of purely functional usage. Beautiful ceramic tiles rose to dado height on staircases and corridors and were complimented by hardwood joinery and superbly crafted handrails throughout, all of which would have caused severe damage to the rain forests.

The whole, though, was an absolute rabbit warren of offices and storerooms, and labyrinth and maze of corridors and alcoves which seemed endless and in which I often got lost, especially on my initial stint. It was instilled into this rather naïve fifteen year old that I must knock on every office door and must wait to be called in because, as Dennis said with a twinkle in his eye: "There's all kinds of goings on in these offices." I did lapse, however, on one Saturday morning when I thought no-one would be in work and can confirm there were indeed 'all kinds of goings on in those offices!' Two members of staff spent the rest of their employment with MEB avoiding my glances.

Within the three-storey complex was a quadrangle some fifty feet square on which was sited our small carpenters shop. This small area of land was reminiscent of an oasis. In summer it was ablaze with the purple and white of buddleia and the home of various wild flowers, which had miraculously found their way into this small Eden in the heart of our city. Twice it was the summer home of the comparatively rare Black Redstart and interested office staff could be seen observing our small parcel of land with binoculars from the overlooking office windows. The winter months, however, were less inviting. Our location was cold, dark and sometimes depressing – apart from our gate crashing of the office Christmas parties.

The Birmingham Area Manager was Mr. Emil Braathen, who had been a Dutch paratrooper in World War Two and was, I found, a very nice man. He was a prodigious smoker and indeed the atmosphere in his office was akin to that of the top deck of an inner circle No. 8 bus on a winter's day. As one of the few non-smokers in Britain's work force at the time, I had sympathy with Miss Ashdon, his secretary. Both their signatures adorn my apprenticeship indentures.

Quite often we would be called to do work for Mr. Braathen, ease a door or drawer, replace a sash cord, etc. There were never any moans from the carpenters I worked with; in fact it was a stampede of almost indecent haste to his office. There was an ulterior motive however other than the job itself. For on Mr. Braathen's desk there was a round tin, the contents of which were given away by the label with a sailor's head and the word 'Players'. The manager would always offer us a couple of Players from his tin. To my mates who survived on a diet of Wild Woodbines the offering was manna from heaven, and I, for the benefit of my mentors and the threat of a 'clip round the ear' became a smoker to enhance that offering.

The Dale End complex, as previously alluded to, was larger, almost unwieldy in size and a proverbial nightmare to maintain. After spending a substantial amount of time doing my upmost to help in the daunting task of its upkeep, I would still discover rooms, corridors and niches I had not come across before. Encompassed within these rambling buildings was a very large and important sub-station which served a substantial part of the city centre. It was in the outer area of this building that there was a door, the entrance to a totally unrelated service to that of the mundane supply of electricity. For inside was a broadcasting studio.

I was only allowed inside on a couple of occasions for when the studio was 'live' the room had a security akin to a Churchillian bunker. The studio must have been one of the earliest bases for hospital radio in the city, providing the hospitalised with a 'pick-me-up' of requests, music and good wishes from family and friends. As I recall the service, which was run by volunteers, did not operate on a daily basis, but I know it was very popular with patients and hospital staff alike. The studio functioned into the early 1960s when it had to find alternative accommodation due to the closure of MEB Dale End and its subsequent demolition.

14

A Room With A View

The architect's office in the Dale End complex was on the first floor and had the advantage of over-looking the bustle of Dale End and the more sedately paced Lower Priory. As with the entire complex, the offices were originally designated living accommodation for those wishing refuge with the Young Men's Christian Association. Thus, the architects department was a collection of such rooms, housing not only architects but surveyors, clerk of works and support staff. The main drawing office was located in the Fazeley Street block. The offices always seemed decidedly cramped, they were probably quite adequate when someone had the bright idea of locating them there, but over the years their shelves had become crammed with drawings and dusty folders. Surveyor's equipment, poles and dumpy levels filled every corner and with most of the inmates drawing on pipes, cigarettes and, in the architect's case, cigars the atmosphere could not have been better in a four ale bar!

However, all the impression of crowding, cluster and combinations of tobaccos made these offices, strangely, an exceedingly convivial work place with much banter and pranking. The whole was presided over by a good architect, who dressed befitting his position, immaculately, in pin-striped suits, silk ties and patent shoes. W.R.E.H., his initials, was how he was referred to but to yours humbly, it was 'Sir'.

Strangely while the building department's engineers had a strange relationship with W.R.E.H., he seemed to enjoy the company of the craftsmen he met regularly on the larger jobs which required his input. My craft mentors gladly accepting the offer of a 'Players' but not gaining the cigars which he often smoked.

As part of my training I had the wonderful experience of working with the surveyors for two weeks and greatly enjoyed the opportunity of learning something of the basics of surveying. They were a great bunch who seemed to be on first name terms with the proprietors of coffee shops all across Birmingham. And so for much of that two weeks, if I wasn't out on site I was ensconced in those offices acquainting myself with architect's drawings, reading the various terms and conditions applied to the sites we visited prior to 'pegging out' and enjoying the scene arrayed before me from the large windows overlooking Dale End.

These were most certainly rooms with views. Initially I could not quite understand why my mentors would glance through the window and, chuckling, would make remarks such as; "That was quick, the red head is back" or "Blondie is working today" or "There's a new face" or "He's got some appetite" or "The Humber's here!" I then realised that I incidentally was being acquainted with the goings on at the pub opposite, the Star Vaults. There certainly was plenty of activity at the Star during the midday opening session which beggars the question "What was it like at night?" I never had the pleasure of using the hostelry myself for the pure reason that it was overlooked from the offices by a variety of bosses who took a dim view of a liquid lunch by their manual staff. So if my craft mentors wanted a lunch time pint we exited the site via the rear Moor Street entrance and went to the Lamp.

There could be little extension to our half-hour lunch break however, for we had to negotiate our way back to the carpenters shop via the ground floor offices whichever diversion we took. So it was sandwiches and at the most a couple of pints, whilst it was spit and sawdust at the Lamp, it was comfortable and a decent pint and there was none of the Star's shenanigans!

15

A Handcart Down Henns Walk

As mentioned previously our remit for maintenance at Dale End also encompassed that of Island House, a unique triangular shaped edifice, a short distance away in Fazeley Street. Movement of materials between the various buildings was by virtue of an ancient handcart and usually fell to the apprentice to facilitate. I once pushed that old cart with another lad from Dale End to Bingley Hall laden with materials for an exhibition stand. High Street then New Street, into Paradise Street and Broad Street and back again! I remember thinking to myself, struggling up the New Street incline towards the Town Hall, that I wish Dad had given me a chemistry set to play with instead of a hammer and saw!

It was a drizzly autumn morning when, with the assistance of another apprentice, a very tall, leggy lad who left us well before the end of his six months trial period, we loaded timber, plywood and fixings onto the handcart for a job at the Fazeley Street office. The load was heavy and awkward, but neither of us fancied a second journey so we set out a little apprehensively down Dale End and took the right turn into Henns Walk, a narrow cobbled thoroughfare of about 150 yards, which ran downhill from Dale End to Moor Street. My colleague was proudly shod in a new pair of hobnail boots and they were a major factor in what happened next.

Each holding a shaft of the cart, we started to descend Henns Walk. We were but a short distance into the passageway when my mate discovered that hobnail boots were as skis on snow to wet cobbles. The inevitable slip left him on his back, still holding the shaft, until he could hang on no longer. The cart skewed but my best efforts to pull it to a halt counted for nought as I too landed on the wet cobbles. The cart and its spewing load gathered increasing momentum and careered down Henns Walk, crossed Moor Street and crashed into the pub wall opposite, about twenty seconds prior to a bus crossing the same junction. We sat, opened mouth on the cobbles of Henns Walk surveying the wreckage and contemplating our fate. The ferocity of the kick up the back side that I received from a very irate charge-hand, has meant that at least one citizen will forever remember Henns Walk, which fell victim of the city's 1960s redevelopment.

What became of the handcart? Well, it was still in occasional usage at our Piers Road Depot well into the next decade – but not on the public highway!

16

The Medical
"God heals, and the doctor takes the fee"
G. Herbert

In the first year of my apprenticeship I felt under threat. It wasn't constantly at the forefront of my thoughts, but there lurking in the background like the discomfort and irritation of a mouth ulcer or ingrowing toenail. The pain manifested itself if I thought I had erred in some way. I was only reminded of the fact that I was on trial for that period just once, in hindsight it must have been akin to playing the leading part in a hanging or on a cart to face Madame Guillotine!

One day, shortly before this thought provoking period was reaching its conclusion, I received a letter that I was to attend a medical. I had been booked an appointment at a private practice in Edgbaston. I was slightly disconcerted by the news for I had gone through a cursory examination some twelve months earlier when a doctor, who looked not much older than I, had caused me some concern. He had called out my name, did various basic checks lasting all of five minutes and sent me on my way, only suddenly to call me back telling me to open my shirt again. He reapplied the stethoscope to my chest and sat as though in a trance before waking up and nodding his head. He packed the instrument into its case and off he went no explanation as to why he had taken such an interest in my torso, but it did occur to me that he had found something amiss. It did sometimes come back to me, not thinking that if he had found some abnormality he would surely have told either me or my GP. Anyway, now, according to my peers, I would be having a very thorough medical examination. I did feel in some trepidation that a junior doctor had been indecisive and now a consultant would confirm the worse, whatever that was.

The house, that was the private practice, was as impressive as Edgbaston could get. A large authentic Georgian property with an 'in and out' gravel drive and lawns of shot silk in the July sunshine. They formed a semi-circle inside the gravel drive, a large cedar tree at the lawn's centre, an imposing feature. I stood at the entrance and surveyed a setting that would not have been out of place in a Jane Austen novel. I looked down at my work clothes and dusty shoes, which I tried to embellish with some shine by self-consciously rubbing them on the backs of my grey trousered legs. At the entrance to the house I pushed a highly polished brass bell and took a pace back so as not to be on the top step. The door eventually opened and revealed a lady who gave the impression that I should really have gone to the side entrance, which I am sure that this house would have. Her scrutiny of me was overtaken when her eyes fell on the brown envelope in my hand, which she obviously recognised as the passport to another twenty-five guineas for her employer.

I was beckoned into another world. No lino or distemper here, a deep red carpet which threatened to bury my shoes, antique furniture, lush wall coverings and impressive paintings in ornate, wide gilt frames. I was ushered to a chair and waited to be seen. A view to rear, from what I could see for I was afraid to move from the chair, revealed a garden which appeared to go on for eternity. All was beautifully kept, the house had the not unpleasant smell of beeswax and the highly polished sheen on tables and fittings bore testament to its very regular usage. I sat for, it must have been ten minutes, and took in every nook and cranny – paintings, piece of porcelain, statuette and candlesticks, a very different world indeed.

During those ten minutes the head of the house keeper would occasionally poke around the door to tell me that her employer would not be long, a pretext I think to ensure that I hadn't made off with the 'family silver'. Eventually she called me into another room where a small, silver haired man, sat side on to an open rolled topped bureau. He stood as I approached and held out his hand, a welcoming smile bathed his face. He was immaculate in appearance, a beautifully tailored suit, silk tie and matching handkerchief in his top pocket, shining shoes that my own workhorses could only aspire to. "Have a seat Robert," he said. I felt really comfortable in his presence; he had the reassuring and confident demeanour that was the epitome of a consultant of some standing. Of course the beeswax pervaded the air in the lavish surgery, but I thought I detected just the slightest hint of whisky fumes.

The medical lasted an age and covered nearly every body part from head to toe. Having asked my occupation we chatted happily on the topic of antique furniture, his favourite pastime. To my great relief he said I was "A1, a very fit young man!" No second sounding with the stethoscope! I was shown out to the gravel drive by the poe-faced house keeper, who I thought for a brief moment was going to ask me to empty my pockets of their contents. With both relief and elation I strode down the drive, resisting the urge to take a short cut to the open gates across the pristine lawn. It was 3.00 pm and I contemplated making my way home for an early 'knock off'.

I resisted the temptation and made my way back to my workplace at Dale End. I entered the workshop to find Reg downing the remains of a cup of tea. He nodded his head in my direction and lifted the sleeve on his fawn, light weight summer jacket glancing at his wrist watch:

"I wondered if you would return to work," he said with a rare smile. "Well done lad, no problems I hope?"

Whether by design or not I cannot say, but my decision to err on the side of caution and return to duty had been very much the correct one. I had a sneaking feeling that Reg was thinking that I would not!

17

... A Mighty Man Is He, With Large And Sinewy Hands And The Muscles Of His Brawney Arms Are Strong As Iron Bands

The Village Blacksmith

It was truly frustrating to arrive at Piers Road by 8.00 am in the morning to find yourself journeying back to whence you had already travelled by 10.00 am. Reg was a dab hand at this particular tactic. He would rarely inform us as to his future work plans for his staff, indeed my mentors would often be of the opinion that any planning as to work and Reg's organisation was purely coincidental.

On this particular day I had been paired with old Horace, we had collected our plastic bus tokens, Reg had told us where to disembark from the bus to save the MEB one old penny, I grabbed the tool bag and we were on our way to Bartley Green substation – about twenty minutes' walk from my home. It wasn't a bad location for Horace either for he lived in Cotteridge.

Horace was a great bloke and was in his late 60s in 1961 when, I estimate, this assignment took place. He was the fount of all knowledge with regard to builders on the southern side of the city. He, like many others of his age, had been subjected to life in the depression between the world wars and the hire and fire syndrome that was the building trade at that time. There was nothing special about the Bartley Green job, just general maintenance. However, there were two significant happenings whilst we were at that location and the first came as we arrived at the sub-station, at a brisk walk for the heavens had opened as we alighted at the California Public House from the No. 20 Weoley Castle bus, having supplemented Reg's tokens with one old penny to save a very long walk.

Horace quickly had keys at the ready and as soon as we were inside we headed for the mess room to dry out and have our morning break. As usual I was the bearer of Horace's tools, such was the lot of the apprentice in my days, and I followed him into the mess room. At the table sat a man of Horace's vintage who stood up to greet my mentor: "Hello George, how are you doing?"

George standing was a big presence. He shook hands with Horace and it was then that I noticed George's hands for they were massive, the largest I have ever seen and after all these years they remain so. Horace introduced me and George nodded. As I soon found out he was a man of few words, although he and Horace did have an affinity due to their ages.

"He's a big bloke," I said. Horace nodded:

"Thought you were a 'baggies' fan, that's George Ashmore, Albion and England goalkeeper," he said. "Played for England before the second war."

I had been an Albion fan from the age of about six, encouraged by my much older brother and in defiance of my father who was a Villa supporter and Uncle Harry who favoured Birmingham City. The Sunday morning inquests into the Saturday matches were a feature of the football season in my home. I was chastened by the fact that I had never heard of George Ashmore, but thanks to Horace I did now and I was in awe. Unfortunately George, the Substation Attendant, was not forthcoming on his football career and was, as Horace confirmed the most modest of men. Those hands, however, I will never forget.

The inclement weather dogged the outside work we had to do and so, the interior jobs complete, we were dodging showers and quite a bit of time was spent sheltering in the substation mess room. There are few more frustrating conditions for outside carpentry work than persistent heavy showers which cause hurried stowing of tools and materials, destroying system and routine. It was in one of those enforced, elongated weather breaks, that Horace imparted some of my own family history of which I was totally unaware and, for some reason, had never been shared with me by family members. Both my maternal and paternal grandparents had strong links with Kings Norton in the 19th century. Horace lived about 100 yards from my maternal grandparents in Ashmore Road, Cotteridge. They lived in Midland Road, so Horace knew my mother, uncles, grandfather and grandmother really well. However, I was totally unaware that Horace knew my great grandfather Jones. He had died long before I was born and as a consequence I knew very little about him, apart from the fact that he and my great grandmother had left Wales in the mid-19th century and settled in the then village of Kings Norton which was in Worcestershire until 1911 when it became part of an expanding city. They had three children, Sarah, Fanny and my grandfather, Henry. I knew also that great grandfather was a carpenter and wheelwright, but to my amazement, Horace was a wonderful source of further interesting information about great grandfather's work in the village and his link with Moundsley Hall, to Squire Pelham Lane and to the parish church of Kings Norton, St. Nicolas.

I hope at this juncture I will be excused for lapsing into a few brief paragraphs of relevant family history as imparted to me by Horace, most of which was confirmed by my parents. Masshouse Farm was situated approximately half a mile from the parish church and was where, during the days of Penal Laws against Roman Catholics, members of that faith met in secret and in some danger. It is unclear when Masshouse Farm was demolished, but my guess would be between 1870 and 1880, Masshouse Lane denotes its approximate whereabouts. However, when demolition did take place oak panelling from the farmhouse, some of which bore the mark F/WB 1634, came into the possession of Squire Pelham Lane and was installed in the library of Moundsley Hall. This work was carried out by my great grandfather Jones, who from left over timbers constructed a shelf unit which has been handed down to me, the ancient oak having a wonderful patina. Parts of an open pale oak fence, which defined the western boundary of Moundsley Hall, can still be seen in Walkers Heath Road and was erected by my great grandfather in the first quarter of the 20th century. Squire Pelham Lane died in 1936. In the last decade of the 19th century, various works were carried out to the parish church of St. Nicolas. This included work to the spire which was carried out by my ancestor and the local parish blacksmith.

I began to wish that the Bartley Green task would last forever, for in just a few days Horace had introduced me to an England international footballer, who better still played for Albion, and a huge slice of family history. That gave me an insight into the life and work of my great grandfather, our shared craft and an even greater appreciation of my forebear.

18

Harry And The 'Pea Souper'

Those born post 1960 are unlikely ever to have known the Brummagem version of the 'pea souper'. For those who haven't witnessed or experienced the phenomenon, an explanation is needed. Between autumn and late winter, the 'pea souper' could strike at any time although, thankfully, the trained eye of the city dweller would recognise the symptoms of its coming. This was no ordinary fog; it had the added ingredient of the smoke from the chimneys of thousands of dwellings, many hundreds of factories and the exhausts of an ever increasing amount of motor traffic. This toxic mixture was eventually to be known as smog. Its density caused chaos and disruption and, more often than not, a long walk home in very unpleasant conditions. That then was the 'pea souper' which was to gradually disappear as the smoke factor was all but exterminated by the implementation of smokeless zones, which, over a short time encompassed the whole city.

And so to Harry. He was, when I first worked with him, just three years off his retirement. He had worked for MEB since nationalisation and in appearance was the epitome of the well-dressed artisan. His sharp features were surmounted by the largest of flat caps; the check pattern of which was so large one square was almost the size of the cap. He always, even in the hottest of weather, had a white starched collar, neatly knotted tie, waist coat and watch chain. His black boots were always beautifully clean and, bless his soul, he was the most kindly and generous of men, particularly to those he liked and we got on just fine.

Harry did, however, have his problems. Time had dulled his enthusiasm for the skills he obviously once had. He could talk the hind leg off a donkey and worst of all had a long standing personal feud with foreman Reg. That combination made him vulnerable to Reg's attention and he was singled out for the more menial, and frankly uncomfortable, of tasks with a definite emphasis on fencing work. He was, in fact, past such arduous work, but Harry was a tough old bird and would never give Reg the comfort of complaint. I should also have mentioned that Harry was also easily affected by drink and just a couple of pints of mild would see him lapse into drowsiness. It was vital to keep him on his feet after a lunch time visit to a local hostelry, for if he sat down he would soon nod off. If that was to happen a constant watch was needed and he was extremely lucky never to have been caught. His visits to the pub were actively discouraged by those who worked with him as we could have also been implicated in his demise and therefore we made sure that such indiscretions were comparatively rare.

Harry was working, not far from our depot, in Handsworth New Road, alongside one of the two railway bridges that span that part of the No. 11 Outer Circle bus route. By 10.00 am this particular morning I was working with him, having been despatched to assist Harry by an uncomplimentary Reg, whose comments about my mentor were not appreciated by Harry's workmates. I had walked through the back streets and emerged close to the job near Ninevah Road. The early morning mist was obstinate and refusing to lift, the visibility at noon was no better than at 8.00

am that morning. At lunch time Harry looked gloomily around the surrounding area, "If this stays like this for much longer lad, it will be a real pea souper by 4.00!" By 3.30 Harry and I were stowing away our gear and securing the site. The long intervals between buses passing our work place suggested that the situation was not only confined to Handsworth. I had a long way to get home to Weoley Castle, Harry even further to Hall Green. We waited with some anxiety at the nearest anti-clockwise Outer Circle bus stop for what seemed ages in an ever thickening smog. Harry eventually decided that we should wait no longer, put our best foot forward and commenced a very long trek home. I really did have concerns for him, Weoley Castle was bad enough for me but Hall Green, even if cutting through the city centre, was some trek and Harry wasn't exactly in the flush of youth.

We were approaching the next bus stop when I happened to look behind and there, crawling towards us, were first the lights and then the ghostly form of a No. 11 bus. The bus stopped and we boarded its crowded lower deck. Our admiration for its driver grew as we truly crawled at snail's pace through Winson Green. He must have taken post luck when crossing Dudley Road, for the visibility if anything was worse. City Road is an extremely long road to walk but our bus was reduced to walking speed and, as the difficult junctions at Sandon Road and Hagley Road loomed, a quiet, concerned apprehension descended on the bus's passengers. It was a similar sense of foreboding that I experienced some years later as our holiday flight to Spain, in a propellered Vickers Viscount, hit stormy weather over the Bay of Biscay. We all breathed a sigh of relief as we pulled into the bus bay at the Kings Head public house at the commencement of Lordwood Road, Harborne. This was a 'clocking in' point for the Outer Circle buses and an inspector was leaning against the clock as we pulled in. We could see an animated conversation twixt inspector, driver and conductor. There were nods all round and the conductor announced to all that the bus would not be going any further than Acocks Green garage. He dutifully altered the destination boards to reflect the change and our bus slowly made its way towards Harborne and Selly Oak, where I would disembark. The journey to the latter took well over an hour, the buses from Selly Oak to Weoley Castle had stopped running and so I walked the rest of the way to my home.

Next morning the smog had done its worst and had deserted Birmingham in the face of a rising, brisk north-easterly wind. Harry, always an early bird, was on site when I arrived at 7.45 am. "What a night," I said, "did you get home alright?" Harry beamed and then related that by the time the bus reached Billesley he was desperate to relieve himself. He told the conductor of his problem and hopped off the bus and gratefully and discreetly made use of a nearby roadside tree. He then trotted down the road and, to the cheers of the lower deck, jumped back onto the same bus. He arrived at his home at 7.30 pm.

I do remember, however, one walk from the city centre, in smog, whilst working in Dale End. I arrived at the terminus of the Weoley Castle buses in Suffolk Street where a long queue was waiting. A bus inspector eventually arrived to tell of the demise of the buses on our route and we all commenced our journey on foot. People walked in groups, complete strangers, but the camaraderie and humour between us was really good. By the time we reached California my walking companions had reduced to four. We were making good progress when we were alarmed by a sudden scream and cry for help. One of our quartet had disappeared down an unmarked excavation. We set to and pulled him out, drenched and covered in mud, and thoroughly disgruntled. The unscathed members of the group were very sympathetic but it was extremely difficult to stifle the laughter which accompanied his very muddy rising.

I know not who conceived the idea of the 'clean air act' but people in cities everywhere in Britain should be eternally grateful to whoever it was!

19

"What's This White Stuff?"

In 1960 immigration from the West Indies to Britain was probably at its height. My morning walk down the Soho Road to Piers Road reflected that trend, for an ever increasing number of people of Afro-Caribbean origin were to be seen.

Handsworth was, of course, the destination of many immigrants to the city. Its large Victorian and Edwardian houses and rows of terraces provided rented rooms and bedsits and the opportunity, with time, of a cheap purchase. The Midlands Electricity Board, at that time, was a very clannish organisation. Many families had their working roots in what was, before nationalisation, the City of Birmingham Electricity Supply Department, and having a relation employed there was a major stepping stone when seeking employment in the industry and particularly in Birmingham.

So it was somewhat of a shock when the new carpenter and joiner who walked into the joiners shop in the spring of 1960 was an immigrant from the West Indies. The newcomer was smiling and had a firm hand shake but, as he in our very long friendship has often recalled, he had a deep foreboding, even fear. I could even, at my comparatively young age, guess the impact on some of our staff. The word 'racist' was a product of later, though not much later years. Most people, though, could recognise hatred. Now when I look back I am filled with disgust with man's intolerance to others especially a fellow worker and a fellow tradesman. It does no good to re-open old wounds and the main perpetrators of the discomfort that, I am pleased to say, were numbered on one hand, have long since gone.

The new carpenter was Hubert and, in a very short time, the smile and firm handshake had stood him in good stead, he had won many friends and gave more back than he took but in a more subtle and often comic way. He did, however, have three very important friends in Jim Slade, Building Superintendent, who himself did not have many friends, Reg and Bert and all but one of the carpenters and joiners.

Hubert found that settling in the 'promised land' was not easy. There was no 'milk and honey' and the pavements were not paved with gold. He had left his wife and child in Jamaica and found a home that was a non-too desirable bedsit about half a mile from Piers Road. It must have been a thoroughly miserable time for him but his smile and good humour saw him through. What did break-down barriers though was his passion for cricket. For Hubert had grown up through the golden years of the game, in the West Indies, during the heydays of the 'Three W's', Worrell, Walcott and Weekes and of Valentine and Sonny Ramadhin, and he would relate tales of these greats as he recalled his days at Jamaica's Sabina Park. That was not all, however, that gave him some esteem among his new workmates for Hubert was reliable in the extreme, hardworking, possessing skill, punctual and – he was left handed! If you worked as a team a 'caggy handed' carpenter was worth his weight in gold. So, despite the initial setbacks, Hubert became very much part of the team and commenced an employment that was to last until his retirement at 65. I worked with Hubert on very many occasions and got on really well with him. When I became his foreman that relationship never changed for he was a valuable and amenable asset.

In the early winter of 1961 Hubert and I were despatched to a job in Kingstanding. Kingstanding was known in the building trade as the Siberia of Birmingham. It earned this title, given to it when the vast council housing estate was built in the 1930s, for being entirely exposed to the chill east wind and the inclement weather it produced. In fact the next highest land to the east is the Ural Mountains of Russia and the temperatures for Hubert and I could have been that of a Russian winter!

It was quite obvious that Hubert had never experienced such cold and, if it hadn't been for our brazier, coke, old timber and a succession of warm drinks, hyperthermia could have resulted. The east wind was cutting, grey skies loomed up over Barr Beacon and flurries of snow were dancing to the tune of the wind.

Hubert stood transfixed, his eyes gazing to the heavens, "What's this white stuff?" he asked.

"That's snow Hubert," I said. "Have you never seen it before?"

"Well only on Christmas cards," he said. "It's a pity it has to be so damn cold for it to happen!"

And so my friend of half a century had an initial introduction to a typical English winter. He soon was to find out the extremes of the season, with the ferocious winter of 1963.

I can recount, however, one particular job with Hubert, strangely again at Kingstanding, when the summer sun beat down on our exposed work site for the whole of three days.

In that unenlightened time if you had a tan you were considered to look fit and healthy. If you covered up against the sun rays you were somehow thought to be 'a bit of a wimp', well that was the philosophy of most outdoor workers. I certainly had exposure and I could literally feel the heat coming from my face and head. At the end of the second day Hubert expressed concern as to the redness of my face and body. "You look as if you are cooking, lad, I don't have that trouble," he said.

"No, you are overdone," I replied. We were still laughing as we boarded the bus at the end of the working day.

Working with Hubert was always a pleasure, although we spent much time laughing, productivity never suffered and it indeed enhanced our working mode. Eventually the MEB gave Hubert the opportunity to learn to drive and in due course he passed his driving test. I well remember his first adventure onto the city's roads, for I was designated on that particular day to be his workmate. I, of course, at that time was a non-driver.

Our conveyance was an elderly Commer van, with an unusual gear change on the steering column. Hubert was advised to practise gear changing around the depot roads before venturing onto the Queen's highway, which he did. As I climbed aboard he explained that, despite his short practise, he was less than confident about our venture.

Within a short distance of the gates of Piers Road we encountered the extremely steep St. Michael's Hill, surmounted at its summit, the junction with Soho Road, with traffic lights. As Hubert tentatively approached the lights they changed to red. Hubert obeyed the signal. However, when the lights changed to green Hubert could not get a forward gear and the old Commer slowly rolled backwards, down St. Michael's Hill with Hubert frantically shifting the gear stick to a variety of positions as our speed accelerated. I was all for decamping when Hubert suddenly decided his brakes would perhaps be a better option. We both heaved a sigh of relief as Hubert composed himself.

"Thank goodness you remembered the brakes," I said.

"Thank goodness there was nothing behind," replied Hubert.

"There was, luckily the driver behind soon found his reverse gear!" I informed him as we both collapsed in a mixture of laughter and relief.

To Hubert, Birmingham is well and truly his home, unfortunately the retirement which should have been spent with his lovely wife, Agnes, never happened. The loss of Agnes at such a tragically young age affected him deeply but he can always be counted on for a smile and a firm handshake. That says much of the man.

20

"Sorry Lad, You Will Have To Do It, I Have Had A Few Pints In The Eagle!"

Just around the corner from the Piers Road Depot in Benson Road was the 'local' – the Black Eagle. It was the epitome of a small Victorian Pub which were common place in districts that had evolved in that era. Rows upon rows of small terraced houses, interspersed with the corner shop and the corner pub.

The Eagle had remained unaltered by progress and still possessed a Tap Room. At lunch times near to pay day it was mainly occupied, work permitting, by carpenters gasping for a quick pint or two. We did have to be quick too, for we only had a thirty minutes break. If we were lucky we might prevail on one of the drivers to drop us round there.

The tradition had started after Bert had retired, not that he would ever do anything to curtail the innocent enjoyment of his fellow working man. It was more the case that he held the view that there was a time and place for everything, and the need to focus on what paid the bills was paramount.

Such social activities impinged on the work element and Bert's ethic. Everyone respected him and his ideals and nothing would be done to complicate his own dedication and duty as joiners shop charge-hand.

It was true to say that we had some champion imbibers amongst my mentors, but all had the sense to call a halt before they were overtaken by the urge for more. Another factor, of course, was the impracticality of finding somewhere to release the intake! Pubs closed at 2.30 pm and suitable places to go, especially in the suburbs, were difficult to find.

On this particular day and at 12.55 pm Dave had gone to his locker, knotted his muffler round his neck, and jerked his way into his donkey jacket, "I'm going for a pint, lad. You're in charge." He was right, there was just Dave and me and he had made his intention clear. I was quite surprised to see him go for it was a chilly autumn day, and an already strong wind was gaining in ferocity and increasing volumes of clouds were scampering across the sky. But then Dave was full of surprises.

I settled into the chair at the end of my bench with tea, sandwiches and the morning paper. I looked at the clock it was 1.40 pm and no Dave which was very unusual for him, but all hell would break loose if he was caught at this time coming back from the Eagle. At 2.00 pm a breathless and red faced Dave crept into the shop and quickly rid himself of muffler and coat, "Sorry lad got into a bit of an argument about the war and got carried away."

I knew Dave by this time very well, and his lack of concentration at his work and frequent visits to the toilet meant that he had taken a lunch time overdose, not vastly but enough to impair his usual sharp mind. It was quite obvious that he couldn't wait for the clock to be pushing round to knocking off time.

His untold wish was gradually coming true when the joiners shop door bounced open and in walked Dennis who had taken over foreman's duties twelve months earlier on the retirement of Reg. There was a marked contrast in styles, Reg was all hustle and bustle, and Dennis gave out a sort of detached air of competence and calm, in the mould of the much loved John Le Mesurier character, Sergeant Wilson. It was unusual to see Dennis at 4.00 pm in the afternoon in the carpenters shop, and Dave witnessed his entrance with some foreboding. Had his lunch time activity been reported to Dennis?

"Right lads, emergency OT." (overtime)

Dennis never asked if you could work over, it was put in such a way that refusal would be seen as a personal slight to him, the department, the MEB and the whole of the electricity supply industry. At this particular moment in time, and guessing he was off the hook, Dave would have co-operated with this worst enemy. An upper storey window had fallen out of a derelict property owned by the MEB in Parker Street, Ladywood. The window casement had been forced off its hinges by a strong wind and landed in the street below, fortunately without injury to either individual or property. We had to make safe the three upper windows overlooking the street. Then Dennis uttered the words I was dreading, "You will need a double extension ladder." I looked at Dave, yes I thought, in your condition I know who will be climbing it! I looked out of the window and could see two poplar trees suffering severe bends in the gale and I cringed. We put together a bag of tools, a nail box with fixings and removed three sheets of plywood from the stores. Sid the driver, with his long based lorry, ladder like a tank's gun lashed to the 'H' frame and over the cab, stood waiting in his blue issue gabardine mac, cigarette perched on his bottom lip and flat cap pulled low to his eyebrows.

"Whose going up the ladder in this then?" he said with a broad grin. Good bloke Sid but I felt his humour was extremely cutting in this instance. Dave had already nodded in my direction.

Every one of my mentors knew that ladders were something I dreaded, Dennis certainly did, but he wouldn't have thought Dave incapable of doing the ladder work and I was in no position to say "Not me!" The only bright spot was the added income to be received next pay day, but that was some way off.

Parker Street was an extremely narrow thoroughfare dominated on the city side by derelict buildings and a still operative sub-station that had once been a greater contributor to the system than it forlornly looked now. Sid's Bedford lorry filled the cobbled street, its wheels almost in the gutters on each side. Two wooden barriers were sited at each end of the street, which caused a few heated words with drivers who used that thoroughfare in the rush hour as a 'rat run'. Arguing with the doleful Sid, however, was a bit like throwing a ball at a wall!

The extension ladder was lengthened to its required height for access to the first window, saw benches set up on the cobbles and a sheet of ⅜" plywood ready for cutting to size.

"Sorry lad, you'll have to do the ladder work, I had a few pints in the Eagle."

"Yes," I said, "I know" and I readied myself to scale the ladder that was my equivalent of Everest. My foot was on the bottom rung, my folding rule ready in its overall pocket.

"Where are you going Bob?" voiced Dave.

"To measure up," I said.

"No need lad, I can do it from here and save you six journeys.

Dave studied the three windows and marked out the ply for cutting. "I'll do the cutting lad, you do the fixing and Sid will foot the ladder." Surely he can't be having a guess at the size, not Dave, I thought. The first piece was cut and the splintered edges on the cut sides sanded smooth. I tucked my claw hammer into my bib and brace overalls, 2" nails into my pockets and placed the plywood against the ladder and slowly went my way, raising the ply as I went.

"Best of luck, lad," said the cheerful Sid.

The higher I ventured the stronger the wind seemed to gather. The narrow street and high buildings on either side making a tunnel effect but yours truly, on a ladder with a piece of plywood, was less than aerodynamic. If this ply doesn't fit, I thought, and I have to come down again, I will not be happy. I reached the top of the ladder and pushed the plywood's bottom edge onto the cill, pressed against the face of the ply – a perfect fit with just a bit of tolerance. Leaning against ladder and plywood and holding onto nothing, I hammered home nails which only just gripped in a frame in the initial stages of decay. I descended the ladder without a word, trying desperately to hide my fear and there, waiting for me, were the other two pieces of ply!

The job was completed and inside the relief and pride that I had conquered my fear in appalling conditions was unparalleled. Sid laughed, "well done son, I could see your legs shaking from down here."

"The next time you go up a ladder, just remember this job and it will be a piece of piss," said Dave and he and Sid choked on their Woodbines.

"Come on Dave, how did you do it?"

"Do what?" said Dave, knowing full well what I meant.

"Calculate the size of the ply," I said.

He laughed.

"Just measure a brick, add the joint and just count allowing for clearance. If you can't trust Victorian and Edwardian craftsmen, you can't trust no-one!" he explained.

We boarded Sid's lorry and headed for Piers Road, it was approaching 6.00 pm and we were sat in the traffic at Spring Hill.

"I could have gone home from Parker Street," I said.

"Yes," said Dave, "or you can sit here with me and Sid in this horrendous traffic jam at time and a half!" The logic of the man never failed to amaze me.

As a point of interest when Health and Safety legislation was introduced ladders were deemed a means of access to a working area and NOT a working platform. Perhaps whoever drafted the legislation happened to be in the vicinity of Parker Street one windy evening and saw a terrified youth struggling at the top of an extension ladder and realised the dangers!

21

"You Have To Put That Fire Out!"

1963 was one of the worst winters on record. Snow, ice and freezing temperatures lasted for days, for weeks and months on end. A monotonous succession of the same, that even children found boring, and no longer a force of fun.

In the late December of the previous year I had played football, in a cup tie, the match ending in a goal-less draw. The replay took place in the following April! An indication of the longevity of that particular freeze! Unlike much of the building industry who, unfortunately, were laid off, we had plenty of internal work although any further elongation of the inclement weather would have put a severe strain even on that avenue.

However, some external work was pressing and so to an unforgettable job in Shakespeare Drive, Shirley to which Dave and I were despatched. Realising that the 'lads' normal mode of travel to site, on the back of a lorry, would have resulted in a severe case of hypothermia with frostbite complications, I was squeezed into the middle of the cab, handbrake between my legs and immovable. Trapped between Bernard and Dave expounding their memories of an even worse winter, 1947, and almost choking on a fog that only two people smoking Woodbines in an enclosed space could generate, it was a long way from Handsworth to Shirley!

It was always a pleasure to work with Dave, and although others could find him hard going, we got on really well. We both were under no illusions that this particular task, which would have been the proverbial 'piece of cake' in summer months, would be taxing and very uncomfortable.

The site, when we eventually arrived, was on an exposed area near the junction of the main Stratford Road. It had been pegged out by the Architects Department but the pegs with their red painted tops were hidden by the snow. The plan gave measurements from adjacent buildings to one side of the site, but for those co-ordinates I doubt we would have found the pegs until the thaw set in.

Our site boundaries defined, we set up our primitive amenities which by today's enlightened legislation would be totally unacceptable. Our only shelter was provided by two arched wooden frameworks which were tied together at their apex with sash cord. A large tarpaulin was then draped over the arch and held at ground level with a row of house bricks. A large wooden tool box, with padlock, doubled up as a seat. It was a very tight squeeze and you got to know your workmates very well!

Some employers' philosophy in those days was 'If you want to keep warm – work'. Our only form of heating was a brazier, which was fed by what should have been a ready supply of coke, but our provision was often meagre for the conditions and no-one could quite work out why. At this point we should recollect an earlier chapter and Taffy, a driver, who I promised more of later, that point has now arrived.

Piers Road Depot always had a plentiful supply of coke. Various situations determined that this should be so, prevailing weather conditions were of course a major factor. There was a genuine concern for the welfare of operatives, some of whom were getting on in years. Also a realisation that facilities were far worse than those on large building sites and that some form of warmth was needed to dry damp work wear and for the staff to be able to make a fusion of hot beverage.

Thus standard procedure when an outside job was to commence was to determine, not only the material aspects, but also the welfare element and as a matter of course six hundred weight of coke was duly loaded as a starting amount. The load was gauged using a one hundred weight sack, and then emptied loosely onto the lorry for tipping on site. Subsequent loads were ordered via telephone or on a foreman's visit to site.

The job at Shirley was scheduled to last for two weeks, but the onsite conditions make this target out of reach and a further week was required. Excavating the frozen ground was a laborious task which certainly upped our body temperature.

After two days our supply of coke was dwindling fast and Dave telephoned for more and it arrived the next morning and Taffy tipped it as directed. Dave looked at our quota and expressed his doubts as to the amount that had been delivered. This triggered an argument between my mentor and Taffy the driver, which resulted in the latter jumping into his cab and driving off in a huff. Dave was seething and his disposition was made worse when a stronger than normal gust of wind tipped the tent forward, the apex falling onto the brazier. This was a common occurrence and required swift action if our 'home' and possessions were not to be lost.

Dave strutted off to the phone box at 'knocking off' time, I followed and waited outside whilst a one sided argument ensued with Reg. It terminated when the receiver was slammed down and a red faced Dave kicked open the telephone box door with his foot.

By the end of the next day it was obvious that our fuel would do well to last another one. A calm Dave telephoned for more coke and he was told to expect delivery in two days! He remained at peace with himself and, surprisingly, with me.

Next morning we arrived on site as usual and I was to get the brazier going, we had a few shovels of coke left. The kindling was well lit when Dave came over to the fire with a pile of new 6' feather-edged boards and proceeded to break them up. I looked but dare not say anything when he was in this frame of mind. The boards had been pre-treated with creosote and he piled them onto the fire. The smoke billowed and drifted across the main Stratford Road in which was, of course, the rush hour. It was but a matter of minutes before a police car arrived.

"Sorry lads you will have to put that fire out," shouted a police officer from the open window of his patrol car.

Dave went over and explained why we were burning what we were and after his explanation the police officer kindly went to the telephone box with Dave to voice his concerns to the general foreman, Jack Trigger. Two hours later twelve hundred weight of coke arrived, its arrival coinciding with a huge grin on my mentor's face.

And so back to Taffy – apparently ours wasn't the only job to be short-changed with coke supplies although certain traders in Hockley had, I believe, received supplies of our coke. Thereafter coke was delivered in dedicated one hundred weight sacks and all of a sudden we all had a correct and equal quota. I suspect a nice little earner was lost by someone!

Whenever I pass Shakespeare Drive sub-station now, I can still picture the artificial fog we created and a kindly helpful 'copper'. God bless him!

22

"Nothing To Do Lad?
Get Those Hands Out Of Your Pockets!"
And The Winter Of '63

It was a cardinal sin for an apprentice to be caught with his hands in his pockets. We all knew that any one of our foremen or charge-hands would take a very dim view of such a scenario.

I had only just made it to work on time. The No. 11 outer circle bus had braved the harsh winter conditions from Selly Oak to Handsworth, albeit at times reduced to an almost snail's pace. I had run, as best I could in the snow and ice, from Boulton Road, down the Soho Road to our depot and arrived just on the right side of 8.00 am.

I had hung my coat and donned my overalls. My hands were freezing and I suppose my natural reaction was to warm them in my pockets. It was 8.15 am, late for Reg, when the workshop door opened and he stormed in. I didn't realise it but I was caught and his demeanour, which wasn't good at the best of times, was vented on me.

"Nothing to do lad? Get those hands out of your pockets and wait here for me!"

I had finished a job and would have been asking Bert for another but I knew Reg's moods and any explanation would be a waste of time and so awaited the inevitable punishment.

As mentioned before, we were fortunate to have work for much of the building industry had ground to a halt under the tortuous, prolonged weather conditions. Just as we thought we would be next Reg could be relied on to conjure up work and as a consequence we were unaffected.

Reg completed his morning round and returned eventually to me.

"Come with me lad."

I followed him to a storage room which had once, in the distant past, been office accommodation. The room was full of office furniture of differing types and ages, some items looked almost Dickensian, and one could picture the young Copperfield transcribing letters with quill pen in wonderful copperplate writing.

"Being as you've got nothing to do lad, you can repair that lot."

That will teach me, I thought.

"Good experience lad, anything you want see Bert."

I turned to ask – but like a zephyr he had gone. The room had a small, and befitting its contents, an antiquated electric fire which, amazingly, worked. I was grateful for that for it was very cold and the two large sash windows were frozen over which made the room very dim. Three single bulbs hung from an off white ceiling and without that artificial light it really would have been very dingy and uncomfortable. There was no need ever to remind me again to keep my hands out of my pockets.

I stood and contemplated my enforced assignment for a considerable time. I was grateful that the onerous and tedious duties of the youngest apprentice were now in the capable hands of one younger than I, for I thought that this task would require my full attention if it were to be finished by 1964. And so I commenced – desks, chairs, shelf units, tables and bookcases.

On my own, wandering back to the workshop for breaks, materials or the advice of my mentors, I actually began to enjoy the variety of repairs that the differing items presented me with. Bert taught me very passable basic upholstery, a skill I haven't forgotten and I would trudge to a little shop on Hockley Hill for materials, kapok stuffing, gimp and gimp pins, Rexene and upholstery tacks. I often wonder if this 'punishment' was the instigator of the restoration work that I have always enjoyed doing.

Reg would pop in and see me from time to time, but I would give no indication of course that the work was anything but the punishment he envisaged.

By the time the work was completed the worst of the elongated winter had gone and the roads and pavements were almost as treacherous with slush, which at night would turn to ice and then back to slush the next day.

The sequel to this story filled me with disappointment and a certain amount of despair. Some two years after the completion of my punishment I arrived into the depot from a job to find a large bonfire burning in the yard – a bonfire made of obsolete office furniture. Reg had retired by then but, if he had still been around, I would have told him that my real punishment was seeing my hard and rewarding work devoured by the flames on someone's whim. Reg was a craftsman too and I am confident that he would have had sympathy with me. No apprentice of mine ever had time to put their hands in their pockets – that's for sure!

23

Bill The Brickie

One of the good aspects of working in the building trades is the interaction and relationship between different disciplines. As if there aren't characters in my own trade, throw in brickies, plumbers, plasterers and painters and you could easily fill the cast of a Royal Command Performance. Comedians – plenty of them, singers – some of whom were really good and a whole range of speciality acts – not all suitable for regal consumption.

I had never been to Knowle. When I was told by Dave where we were next going to work my first thoughts were that it must be a long way and how on earth I was going to get there?

Somehow my mentor was able to give me the time of a Midland Red bus from the bus station in the city which arrived at Knowle just after 8.00 am. That didn't present a problem as our work base was an MEB shop and the manager could not get there before 8.30 am! Of course, if I had asked Reg I would have probably been advised to walk from the city boundary at Olton!

The Midland Red bus station in the city was a pretty grim place to be in the early morning. The air was thick with diesel fumes. Groups of drivers and conductors stood around in knots, drinking tea and vagrants, aroused from their slumbers, shuffled past on their way to the vibrant markets area for their first pint of the day and the hope of cadging a sandwich. The building was purely functional – it was like an eastern bloc mausoleum, cold, comfortless, without any sort of soul and perhaps, at that time, one of the ugliest places to be in our metropolis.

As far as Olton I was the only occupant of the bus and then it gradually filled and almost emptied again in Solihull town centre. I had little company to Knowle when the conductor informed me that I had reached my destination.

I stood on the platform awaiting my stop and was joined by Dave, from the upper deck, who had boarded the bus at Solihull, unbeknown to me. We crossed Knowle High Street to our workplace and a short time later I looked up and saw a rotund figure ambling towards us and noticed a high grin spread on Dave's face. The two exchanged greetings like long lost brothers, and Dave introduced me to Bill the Brickie.

Bill scrutinised me over heavy framed spectacles. "So this is your lad, then Dave?" he smiled, "nice to meet you Bob." I instantly liked Bill, for when he smiled his whole countenance produced the full works, the one hundred per cent smile which was surely meant and totally unforced.

Bill was wearing a raincoat, muffler and the compulsory flat cap. When his raincoat was removed it exposed a very unhealthy stature. His 'beer belly' overhung a wide leather belt which held up corduroy trousers which dipped under the contours of his pronounced gut. The bottom two buttons of a baggy woollen cardigan had long since given up the battle to stay fastened under the pressure at that point.

Bill's countenance was an extremely flamboyant scarlet and his lips an unedifying purple. As I was to learn he could imbibe copious amounts of mild ale without ever appearing the worse for wear. Those who wished to compete with Bill in the drinking stakes were extremely unwise, and next day certainly wished they hadn't!

Bill had already been on site for a week and had made himself quite comfortable. His subtle humour and endearing conversation had won over the female shop staff, who made his tea at break times. Lunch times, however, their attention was not needed as Bill would make his unhurried way, the short distance to the Red Lion, for his fix of mild ale.

Bill would normally have a brickies mate but due to illness he was on his own. With Dave's permission I was glad to give Bill a helping hand, for his task was a hard one, and while I bashed away at some tough brick work with lump hammer and cold chisel, Bill would take a break. He had two phrases he would use prior to me taking up the 'baton' in the guise of the aforementioned tools. He would look over his glasses:

"Give it the kiss of death, lad!" or "Hit it lad for it has no mother and father!" Bill always thanked me for my toil however small.

Unusually, Bill, a staunch socialist and trade unionist, took the Daily Express, not then a bugle call for the socialist movement. However, there was a reason for Bill's leaning to that particular paper and that was its greyhound correspondent. Bill liked a very moderate flutter and would follow intensely the Express greyhound tips and a dog who ran at Derby called The Bricklayer. Apart from the obvious connection, it seemed that whenever the paper tipped the dog it won and at very good odds. Bill had benefitted financially and so his affinity to the Express was limited to the racing pages and, more importantly, the likelihood of another victory for his favourite greyhound!

Bill's input into the job at Knowle eventually came to an end and he was transferred to pastures new. Some days later

Dave had the need for a lunchtime pint and so we made our way the short distance to the bar of the Red Lion. My mentor was at the counter ordering our drinks when he was approached by a man, obviously a regular by the banter he was engaged in with other drinkers. He spoke to Dave briefly, both men parting with laughter, Dave returning to our corner table.

"Who was that?" I enquired.

"That," said Dave, "was Bill's dominoes partner, asking me where he was. He was devastated when I told him that Bill had gone to another job."

"Why's that?" I said.

Dave beamed and explained that Bill and his partner were a real team and had hardly lost a game for the past two weeks, they were taking on all comers for pints and hadn't had to buy any beer for the whole of that period. Bill would have loved that and I quickly had a mental picture of him, his hand of dominoes resting atop his ample belly and his eyes peering over his spectacles, a foaming pint close at hand in certain knowledge that his long experience and crafty play would be well rewarded with yet another free pint of mild ale.

From then it was just a short time until Bill's retirement and I never did see him after he left but I often think of him. Unfortunately, and perhaps predictably, his retirement was all too short. I hope where ever he is he has access to mild ale, a set of dominoes and the company of the four legged Bricklayer!

24

"May The Good Lord Bless Us And Keep Us"
Whispering Mick

1962 was on the cusp. The sun had not fully risen on a decade that changed so many entrenched concepts, beliefs and ideals. It was an era synonymous with freedom – of expression, of spirit and of love. Chances for me to fully experience the new philosophy, that was seen to have been enjoyed by so many except the working class, were few. If I wasn't at work, I was at college or at home trying to complete college work. Then, all of a sudden, the decade was gone and ninety per cent of the population had either missed it altogether or hadn't the resources to capitalise on it or experience its pleasures.

The exception was the Saturday morning visit to the record shop to spend a fair proportion of our hard earned pittance on a particular top ten favourite. And basically, for me that was that. Those that actually gained most from that period had the financial clout to do so, but then hasn't history determined that that should be so anyway.

One morning, in the aforementioned year of our Lord, a slamming door and the staccato footsteps of Reg heralded his arrival into the joiners shop. To digress a little, some years later I saw in a club in Palma, Majorca, a wonderful Flamenco dancer, clicking heels and snapping fingers – just like Reg. He really did miss a career opportunity there!

"Here," he said. No good morning Bob, how are you son, but then we all were used to that. It was just his way. He stood by me, perspiring even though it was just 8.00 am. He was in his summer garb of a lightweight cream jacket.

"Broughton Road, know it?" he asked. As it happened I did know the road, it was only a short distance from our depot in Piers Road.

"I want you to go with Mick the painter, an electrician has had a mishap with some steps and broken a bathroom window. Help with reglazing and rehang the opening light. There's a ladder being delivered to site." And he was gone.

Mick the painter was short and stocky, red faced with thinning, grey wavy hair. He spoke exceedingly quietly in a broad Irish brogue, inoffensive and industrious and generally loved by all, who had good hearing. I put together a compliment of tools and fixings that I thought would suffice. Mick did likewise and pummelled two pounds of linseed oil putty into a pliable state while I acquainted him with the best way to Broughton Road. We arrived at our work location and Mick knocked the door and rang the bell of a large, rather unkempt Edwardian house. We waited, heard shuffling from inside which culminated in the large panelled door being opened by a blonde, buxom woman in her forties. Her attire was minimal, just a flimsy sky blue nightdress which exaggerated her curvaceous contours. There was an audible intake of air from Mick, probably as loud as if he had spoken and his pipe was only stopped from falling by the abrupt clenching of his teeth. I could feel myself having an extreme case of blushing.

"Who are you?" asked the blonde lady abruptly. Her smile of expectance as she opened the door had quickly evaporated.

Mick was speechless so I blurted out "MEB to repair a bathroom window." She stood to one side in the hallway.

"Sorry, I was expecting someone else. Come through."

We went to the bathroom and then to the rear yard where the ladder lay in wait. Mick had recovered from his shock.

"May the good Lord bless us and save us," he said. "Did you cast your eyes on that Bob?"

"I did Mick," I replied. Indeed after fifty years I still cherish the memory.

There were numerous comings and goings whilst we were there.

"Do you know Bob," Mick uttered in an almost inaudible whisper, "I think this is one of them houses, we best get going as soon as we can!"

I, rather disappointedly agreed, for the inquisitive youth in me would have wished to have seen more of the blonde lady. It was lunchtime when we arrived back at Piers Road and Mick went into much detail of our experience.

His somewhat exaggerated version of events caused much comment and laughter amongst our workmates, but none more so when he described the blonde lady opening the front door in her 'negligence'. Mick did not realise the mispronunciation. It did however cause a chorus of choking on sandwiches and regurgitation of tea through mouths and noses.

Some years later I was at a retirement party where 'Whispering Mick', as he became affectionately known, drank a little too much of the 'Liffy water'. Incredibly we found out that Mick could sing as loud as the next man and at the same time be the life and soul of the party, but that was for one night only.

Throughout my working life I toiled alongside many lads from the Irish Republic, without exception I got on with them all. Their reaction to the indiscriminate Birmingham pub bombings were of disbelief and disgust. They had made their lives in our city, contributed to our city, given their families to our city and witnessed a horror that threatened hard won relationships, friendships and trust. There were those in the short term who could turn their backs on those friendships, but I wasn't one.

25

"See The Conquering Hero Comes! Sound The Trumpets Beat The Drums"
Morrell

There was one omission as regards the various building trades our department employed and that was in plumbing, indeed I was informed it was always so, even prior to nationalisation when the city ran the proceedings.

All matters plumbing were the domain of the very well known, long established company based in Ladywood. They, through a combination of reliability and tradition, were the beneficiaries of a substantial volume of work generated in the Birmingham area. The company was not a large one but coped well with the work load, MEB were always its priority and the basis for its stability and income.

As is often the case, a wide variety of work meant that there were many times when we found ourselves working alongside either Jack or Tony, the plumbing contractor operatives. Personality wise they were chalk and cheese. Jack was a dour Scot in his late 50s; small in stature he had pinched features with a small moustache, not unlike that of the major protagonist of World War Two. He had a very dry humour, bordering on acidic. His workmate, or apprentice, was often the butt of his humour and they had to have broad shoulders to get on with Jack. None of us had ever witnessed Jack without his cap which was a close fitting Kangol type. We wondered if Jack ever went to bed in his adornment, such was his close affinity to the grubby, olive green crown. All else aside, Jack was very efficient in his work and that, very definitely, came first and provided his living, all else was a lesser priority. Not much fun to be had with Jack then, but his fellow plumber was an entirely different character.

Tony was the boss's son, and his philosophy was to enjoy work and try to impregnate everyone in close proximity with his same happy go lucky ethic. He was in his early 30s, extremely extrovert and friendly, the proverbial life and soul of the party. Tall, dark and handsome, the ladies loved him and he knew it. Indeed in some ways his persona when dealing with the opposite sex was really quite outrageous. I, with my quite inexperienced and naïve ideals, would redden with his very forward comments and double meaning chat up lines. What I couldn't quite understand was if any other male had used such rhetoric he would have received short shrift or be the recipient of a well-aimed slap. As soon as Tony walked onto a job, either office or shop, we would start speculating which member of the female staff would fall to his charms and be added to his conquests. A list that we believed was of some length.

From morn to evening there was a continuous flow of jokes, one liners and side splitting comments about other members of the work force, of which young lads like myself, were easy prey. Tony was forever matching us up to one or another office junior causing much embarrassment to both parties and he would enjoy enormously the uncertainty and consternation he caused. How we all kept our concentration on our work I don't know, more of a miracle was how Tony managed to do his.

There was, however, one thing about which Tony was deadly serious and that was his musical talent. In his rare moments of contemplation he would whisk out a set of drum sticks from his overall pocket and enter a trance like state, practising tarradiddle and paradiddle and nodding his head to an unheard beat. This was Tony the freelance drummer, his night job. It was something he was very good at and a roll call of the various bands that co-opted his services was very impressive. Ted Heath, Joe Loss, Kenny Baker and those wonderful bands of the middle years of the 20th century were the recipients of Tony's prowess. He must have been good for they kept him very busy with bookings.

Unfortunately for our extravert plumber, his particular affinity with the opposite sex at one MEB showroom was noticed by a member of management, who took exception to his closeness to a female member of staff. I actually witnessed the incident. Tony playfully crept up on one of the more mature ladies as she was repositioning a Hoover Twin-Tub.

His hands went to her waist and he whispered in her ear, there was no protest from the lady who flushed slightly, smiled and gave our Romeo an unconvincing elbow. Watching Tony though was, if anything, a bigger Lothario renowned for his womanising and unwelcome advances. A big disadvantage for this fellow, however, he was not of the same handsome ilk as our boy and it was obvious, through either jealousy or inferiority, who had put the knife into Tony.

The outcome was that he was kept away from our work and we all genuinely missed him – but none more so than the legions of female staff who had fallen for this charming plumber and drummer!

26

"You Might Think You Are The Boss"

Mr. Slade, his Christian name was Jim but no-one dared to call him that name, was the Building Superintendent. He hailed from Bootle near Liverpool and was brusque, grey haired, red faced and rotund. He didn't suffer fools easily and terrified the life out of many of his staff.

I wasn't terrified of Mr. Slade, I respected him and had witnessed a side to him that few realised, caring and compassionate. He had once saved me from an almost certain sacking after an incident with my charge-hand in which I threw a box of screws, left the job and went home.

I was summoned before him the next day. Everyone I met before my interview had already predetermined my fate; they shook their heads, asked me what I would do now and had I another job to go to. Indeed by the time I had entered his office and stood before him with an air of expectancy matched only by those facing the ultimate end, I had all but given up hope of retaining my apprenticeship and the job I loved.

Mr. Slade had the sternest of demeanours. He slowly drained his cup of tea and, without looking directly at me, asked: "Why did you do it lad, I have heard everyone else but not you?"

That is what I wanted, a chance to explain and Mr. Slade listened to my testimony, his face impassive, until my account had finished.

"You have told all?" he asked. I nodded. He sat back in his chair and spoke without his usual gruffness.

"Don't ever walk off a job again lad, no matter what. You have a problem you knock my office door. What has been said stays in this office. I have had a word with others and I don't want a repetition for otherwise you are doing very well and we all want you to do well. Go and see Reg he will tell you which job you are on next."

"Thank you." I said with relief.

"Just heed my words lad," he said as I left his office. As a consequence I had much time for the man, for I am certain my dismissal must have featured in his thoughts.

You may recall in an earlier chapter the difficulties that my West Indian friend and workmate, Hubert, had to overcome in establishing himself and his family in Britain. He received considerable support from Mr. Slade, help he has never forgotten.

Our boss lived in a flat above the MEB shop on the Stratford Road at Shirley. It was a nice little flat and his wife was manageress of the local Woolworths store which was a couple of retail outlets away. Old Dave had a certain affinity for the showroom for he enjoyed working there, mainly because of its proximity to his home, close to the city boundary at Robin Hood and only walking distance away. It wasn't an easy location for me to work from my Weoley Castle home, three buses away in fact, but I also enjoyed working there. The staff of three and a cleaner were always good to us and as such we made a major refurbishment we had to undertake as painless as possible for them.

I can't remember the exact date, but I remember the apprentice electrician, who with his mate, worked alongside us, had a copy of Lady Chatterley's Lover, the Penguin version which had created uproar in some circles at the time. Copies were extremely difficult to obtain because of the unparalleled public demand. He would read it avidly every break time and, on completion, he held a secret auction for the book at his youth club and made a very substantial profit.

It was not long after we had completed the showroom renovation that we were back at Shirley replacing the rotten casement windows to the flat. Dave had measured up and made the four replacement windows in the joiners shop. A scaffold had been erected to facilitate the removal and re-fitment of the new upper storey windows. The weather was warm and sunny and Mrs. Slade, on intermittent visits from her work to the flat, would make us tea. A jolly sort, unlike her husband, she would leave it on a tray with digestive biscuits on a plate. Our work on the southern elevation made the impromptu refreshments most welcome. We had seen little of 'the boss'. Dave had a sort of love/hate relationship with Mr. Slade, but I suspected there was an intense undercurrent of mutual respect which was in contrast to their curt greetings and shortened staccato discourse.

We were close to completion, the old window frames had been removed one by one, replaced by the new complete with glazing. Mid-afternoon Mrs. Slade arrived and soon a tray with two mugs of tea appeared but no biscuits this time just two large, fresh cream cakes. We thanked her and tucked in.

"You deserve it, you've been spotless," she said.

Our enjoyment of this unexpected treat was tempered by the sudden and unexpected arrival of her husband. I moved to set down my mug of tea.

"Stay put, carry-on," said Dave.

Mr. Slade ascended the metal staircase to the landing where we were enjoying our afternoon tea. He looked daggers and I could see by the ripples of the tea in my mug that his demeanour recorded some misgiving with me. Dave, however, remained impassive.

"What's this then? You don't have time for tea and cakes!" said Mr. Slade in a very special, extra gruff voice. The front door of the flat opened and Mrs. Slade stormed out. She stood with hands on hips and glared.

"These blokes have done a good job and this is my thanks to them. You are their boss at Piers Road and you might think you are the boss here, but you aren't!"

Smiles on Mr. Slade's face were rare but this was one occasion. He slapped Dave on the shoulder. "Enjoy your cakes," he said.

Dave was still laughing as Mr. Slade entered the flat.

"Our lives won't be worth living if she hasn't bought him one of these cakes," he said.

My saviour retired, moved away from Birmingham and died before his time. A little bit of me died also, for without his compassion and understand I doubt I would be relating this story now. Never judge a book by its cover, however churlish it may appear.

27

Truly A Most Unseemly Sight!

In many ways I was quite sad that I missed out on my country's call to serve as a national serviceman. In fact I missed the calling by several years for in any case due to apprenticeship my call up would have been deferred until the age of twenty-one. There are many who enjoyed the experience and quite a few who regarded the whole happening as a complete and utter waste of time.

One such individual was Dave's son who I first met in the summer of 1963, when he turned up one day at our worksite at Water Street sub-station in the city. He was on leave and could not have been more disparaging of his current lot in life. I really thought it surely could not have been that bad but for someone with a highly active and articulate mind; his boredom with the whole set up was genuine.

Water Street sub-station was a large rambling building which had, in its heyday, been a major cog in the generation of electricity for a large section of the north-eastern parts of the city centre which included most of the Jewellery Quarter. Water Street itself was a dead end, the large gates of the sub-station entrance blockading any further progress of its cobbled surface. The building also had an entrance through gates which faced St. Paul's Church and the square which was named after the church. I quite liked working at Water Street it was easy to get to, a ten minute walk from the terminus of my bus, the whole area then a far cry from how it looks now. It had character in abundance. A grimy old fashioned character of workshops, of alleys and doors hiding an abundance of skills and treasures and of course, the ultimate treasures – the St. Paul's Tavern and the church whose true splendour remained hidden with a build-up of dirt and dust dating back to the industrial revolution.

As its street name suggested, water wasn't far away. The canal ran parallel and adjacent, separated by a row of terraced cottages and a high wall within the sub-station yard. A good view, however, was available from the former workshops on the upper floor. A series of locks on this stretch of the cut took barges and narrow boats to and from the hub of the city's network at Gas Street basin. It was, again, a far different site in 1963 as the whole waterway system in the city was in a very sorry state then, decrepit, unloved and rundown.

So why were Dave and I at Water Street on this occasion? Water Street sub-station, which hadn't contributed to the generation of electricity for many years now, was formally to be recognised for its past contribution and be de-commissioned, the last of its type in the city. A brief survey of the site had determined what was required to spruce up the old sub-station and its sparse amenities to facilitate a visit from the upper echelons of MEB and civic guests from the city, including the Lord Mayor. It was then the task of Dave, me and two painters to achieve a near miracle in transformation and hallucination in just two weeks. Muslin drapes of suitable colours were to be hung to form a large tent within the generation room, hiding the muck, grime and deep dust that prevailed throughout the building.

A rostrum and 'control panel' with ceremonial button was to be constructed, the toilet area redecorated and the privy doors altered to remove the nine inch gap at their bottom. I was once comfortably within that essential room when I had a swift visit from a mouse who found the gap under the door too much of a temptation. I don't know who was more surprised – me as I hurriedly tried to pull up underpants, trousers and overalls, or the mouse that quickly scuttled out.

We did, however, have an incentive to do our best to complete by the morning of the ceremony. Catering contractors were to supply a buffet and there was to be a bar. Then it was decided that we should stay on site in case of any hiccups, we were to be invisible though unless there was a problem. Dave was euphoric as he watched cases of wine and crates of M & B Albright ale being offloaded in the area where he had made the bar. The buffet was superb and, for someone who thought that the premier buffet was dished up at my local on darts and dominoes nights, an introduction into how the other half lived! A waitress took me on a tour of the fare – salmon (without its tin), mixed meats (some of which I had never heard of), sausage rolls, crusty batons of bread, coleslaw (which I had never before been acquainted with) and prawns (which I could have easily snaffled there and then and had only ever seen in a book about sea creatures and on a slab in the old market hall).

The dignitaries arrived, the speeches were made, the ceremonial button pressed. The buffet consumed and the bar drunk dry. I would like to relate that Dave and I were party to the celebrations but not a morsel came our way, or even the dregs from a bottle of ale. Dave was downcast and I didn't eat a king prawn for another ten years.

And so we donned our togs to go home, calling at the revitalised toilets on our way. The tail end of the ceremony was still in progress as we opened the door to the toilet block.

There before us was a truly unseemly sight a dignitary on his knees, head over the toilet pan, being violently sick. Dave looked on with an air of disgust. "Greedy sod," he said, "serves him right."

No ale, no prawns but revenge, if only the mouse had been there to see the victory. "Come on son," said Dave, "tomorrow lunch-time in the St. Paul's I will treat you to a couple and sod them!" A smile spread across his face as we turned to see the suffering male emerge from the toilet behind us, face ashen and wiping vomit from his tie.

28

"You Know I Have Sung That Song All Over The World!"

Les Cox

Holidays were sparse in 1959, as indeed they were for the whole of my apprenticeship, which I think gave all workers at that time a greater appreciation of Bank Holidays. Those few days through the year that are historically linked to the Christian religious calendar and are instrumental in providing precious time with loved ones, and for those of faith to fully empathise with their beliefs.

The spring and summer bank holidays were for many an escape from the mundane, the drudgery and the everyday monotony of ordinary working class life. Coach companies preyed on the culture with day trips to Weston Super Mare, Rhyl, Barry Island and Blackpool. There was also the compulsory mystery evening trip which was a mystery only in the fact that it was pot luck between Worcester, Stratford-upon-Avon or Evesham. It was a release and a chance for fathers and grand-fathers to drink in a different pub and partake of a different beer, whilst the rest of the family did the sights and enjoyed a cruise down the Severn or the Avon. The journey home always featured a 'free and easy' of old favourites, resurrected by tipsy parents who you couldn't get to hum any other time. Comfort stops were frequent, it mattered not where or the provision. The driver always being appeased by a collection which was compulsory.

Railways too offered 'Joe Public' the same opportunities and excursions to destinations further afield than practical for the motor coach which saw the platforms at New Street, Snow Hill and Moor Street crowded with expectant and happy throngs. Christmas remained aloof among bank holidays, a time for family, for friends and a time for those away from home to return on Christmas Eve, an irresistible magnet pulling hearts to the core of their lives and families.

With mid-December approaching my workmates began to give out the symptoms of being 'demob happy'. An air of wonderful expectancy pervaded the work place and even the grumpiest of my artisan mentors could be heard lapsing into the occasional carol with rarely used artistic prowess. The closer we got to the twenty-fourth the more amiable everyone became, be they my colleagues, the bus conductors, neighbours who wouldn't normally give you the time of day, milkmen, bakers and even the coalman's horse seemed to trot with the aplomb of a Derby winner. A very happy time of year.

What of the humble apprentice? Well clips round the ears were less, as were kicks up the backside and 'rollickings' were given with a smile. For the first three years of my apprenticeship my bank holiday would commence at 12.00 noon on Christmas Eve when my elders would decamp to a favourite hostelry and I would make my way home, grateful for an extra half day's holiday. Of course, I had a good idea what my mentors were up to, but until I was finally invited to accompany them I had not thought that such copious amounts of mild ale could be drunk by so few. I had enough money – just about, for one round which was quickly and graciously devoured by my mentors. I had done my duty however, and strangely felt somehow quite proud. By throwing-out time it was difficult to recall anything but that it was a thoroughly good time.

The inn which benefited from this Yuletide extravagance was very much determined by where the majority of the staff were working. I cannot remember a Christmas Eve, however, where one location suited all the department's trades. More often than not carpenters and joiners, bricklayers and mates and painters were appointed different pubs, no malice, just convenience.

For each depot in the Birmingham Area there was a favourite pub. For the Handsworth Depot it was the Black Eagle; for Summer Lane, the Woolpack. At Dale End the White Horse in Moor Street, for Kings Heath the Hazelwell, Bordesley Green the Avenue, Solihull the Greville Arms and Chester Street the Golden Cross. All are remembered with affection and some I have made a point of returning to as years have gone by. The experience hasn't always been a happy one, but then fifty years is a long time and pubs must cater for the needs of today's clientele.

Leslie Cox was an ace. A bricklayer by trade and someone I had an awful lot of time for. Les had principles which held him in high regard with his workmates. He was honest, hardworking, good at his job and had strong views on Socialism and Trade Unionism, a natural for taking up the cudgels of his colleagues.

Thus, when the building crafts unions amalgamated Les, who was the bricklayers shop steward, was unanimously elected to oversee us all. He was plain speaking, called a spade a spade, despised the Conservative party and loathed even more the Liberals. He had high integrity and a respect for every hardworking man and yet Les was quite an innocuous chap. Quiet and unassuming, deeply thoughtful and hard of hearing! He mixed easily within a crowd but had fire in his belly that turned to an inferno when someone collided with Les and his ethics. His wizened face would lose its benign countenance, his cap would be pushed back on his head with the peak pointing to the sky and his small frame assumed a giant's proportions, and Les would become his idol – Nye Bevan.

The MEB had a chairman who many employees believed was specifically appointed to cosy up to the workforce after a particularly disastrous period of industrial relations under his predecessor. Not a good appointment, for the gentleman in question had an unfortunate, condescending attitude which aggravated employees even more than his brusque and unbending forebear.

At a general meeting with shop stewards the newly appointed chairman embarked on what proved to be a disastrous question and answer session. There was no shortage of questions but it became evident that the chairman was unwilling to give frank and straightforward answers which began to agitate the union side.

Les had been waiting patiently to put his question. When his moment came he deliberately asked a very pertinent and uncomplicated one, to which a straight response was required. Unfortunately the answer fell well short of expectations and Les felt the matter had been trivialised. Les rose to his feet and delivered a 'Bevanite' broadside of which the culminating sentence was: "I would much rather be laying bricks than listening to an idiot like you!" At which Les picked up his briefcase and left the room, followed by his fellow shop stewards. This happening, however, did not go unnoticed at a higher level, for that particular chairman's tenure in office was extremely short.

Les was the first ordinary working chap I knew to take a cruise holiday. How Les could afford such a luxury on the relatively poor pay our craftsmen received caused much speculation, from an inheritance to a pools win, whatever, Les deserved his holiday of a lifetime and no-one pried into his luck.

Christmas Eve at Solihull Depot meant from noon 'till almost 3.00 pm was spent at the Greville Arms. A good time was always guaranteed for the site of our depot was adjacent to the larger West Midlands Gas headquarters and their staff also frequented the local pub. It was indeed a lively and loud occasion with a crowded assembly room, bar and smoke room, also congested with the pub staff hard pressed to keep pace with the demand.

Eventually a piano lid was lifted and a very competent pianist had stretched his fingers to try and span an octave, adjusted the stool and was manfully trying to keep a succession of Presley's, Cogan's and Sinatra's in tune. It never fails to amaze me that people from the tone deaf to the breathless really think they can sing after a few drinks, and those who are spectators and in the same inebriated state will applaud anything, even encouraging encores, all good fun.

There were a group of six from our department who were clustered around a corner table, thankful that one of our number had been despatched to the pub earlier to lay claim to our precious possession. The company and the conversation were excellent and an all-round convivial atmosphere prevailed. Pint glasses filled our table and a festive odour of a variety of cigar brands prevailed. A succession of pints of mild was bound to have their effect and Les, who had been the instigator of lively and hilarious conversation on a whole range of topics, drifted into a contemplative mood. He seemed hundreds of miles away as indeed he was, he later confided that he was aboard a cruise ship under a Mediterranean sky!

None of us was prepared for what happened next as Les rose from his stool and walked towards the pianist. He leant on the piano in a pose that Noel Coward would have been proud of and, with the aplomb of that gentleman, asked if the maestro knew 'Begin the Beguine?' The pianist nodded in recognition and embarked on a suitable introduction and eventually gave Les his cue. Les sang, but when he reached 'a night of tropical splendour' he suddenly stopped. The maestro carried on playing but poor Les had completely forgotten the words. A sympathetic round of applause followed Les back to a slightly embarrassed table.

He quietly sat down and drained his glass, then as if in a trance, he informed all within earshot, "Do you know lads, I have sung that song all over the world and never ever forgotten the words!" Dave was about to ask if Les could remember now he was back with his mates, it was too late for Leslie's head had fallen to one side, his cap at a jaunty angle and he was sound asleep.

When next I saw Les he was back to his old self, another Christmas over.

"I believe I disgraced myself at the Greville Arms Robert," he said.

"Not really, you just forgot the words to 'Begin the Beguine'."

"Yes," he said, "and do you know I have sung that song all over the world!"

What a trooper, did I miss him when he retired!

29

Nosser, Chocker And Sir Stafford

As I have mentioned earlier, one of the mostly pleasant aspects of working in one of the building trades is the interaction which takes place with other trades.

So it was I found myself with my mentor, Dave, on a job at MEB South-West District Depot at Kings Heath. A major redecoration of the offices was taking place and so a larger than usual contingent of painters were in residence which included three brothers known as Nosser, Chocker and Sir Stafford. These were not their real names of course, but names bestowed upon them by themselves. Nosser, who had a slightly enlarged hook nose, Chocker, the youngest, gained his name by packing into his life so much betting, boozing, womanising and food. He lived an extraordinary full life and died well before his time. The third of the brothers, Sir Stafford, was the eldest, certainly he liked a bet and a pint but he was decidedly more level headed and sober than the other two. Sir Stafford was named after a former Chancellor of the Exchequer, Sir Stafford Cripps. The nickname given to him by the other two, for he had to undertake the not easy duty of rationing out monetary allowances and ensuring that wages could be eked out from payday to payday. This tortuous task would often lead to disputes and for the frugal Sir Stafford his brother's avarice caused much heart searching. Over indulgence was a particular feature of the life of Chocker.

Sir Stafford was in particular someone whom I got on with really well. His speech was slow and deliberate and to every question he gave a great deal of deliberation and thought. His answers were often humorous and often his response was no answer at all. He was always a sage-like figure and a fount of extraordinary wisdom, however convoluted. I once asked Sir Stafford how old he was, he looked over his spectacles, his briar pipe puffed out a plume of smoke and slipped to the corner of his mouth. It was a question that most people would be able to snap an answer to, but not Sir Stafford. The 'pieces of the jigsaw' must be fitted and in place before any further utterance.

"I am very old," he said, "I can remember when Birmingham Town Hall was a barber shop!"

This was an infinitely more intriguing and interesting answer than the one I expected. To him the world moved at a far slower pace and he had an appreciation of time and punctuality that never saw him rushed. In today's parlance he was indeed very laid back, he had none of the hustle and bustle associated with his two brothers; none it seemed had entered his genes.

Sir Stafford's perusal of the racing pages would commence on the purchase of his daily newspaper, his bus journey to work and his morning break. The horses he referred to as nags and the dogs as growlers. His selections, however, stayed within his domain and his losses and winnings were his affair only. Although the activities of Chocker and Nosser I know caused him concern, he never outwardly gave any show of dissent and carried out his role in an almost detached manner.

Nosser was not flamboyant and was in many respects a happy medium twixt his two brothers. Chocker, however, was a real character whose life itself was a tangled web of misdemeanours of a non-criminal variety. He once confessed to me that his private life was a mess, but he never allowed it to detract from what was an outgoing, extravert personality.

By the time I had first got to know the brothers I had also become acquainted, through my solicitor uncle, with Kings Heath dogs. The track closed in 1973, but I discovered through my uncle's teaching, that scrutiny and study, memory and a slice of luck went some way towards finding winners. It was a formula that he found lucrative but was also compensated by the fact that he carried out some legal work for the tracks owners and therefore was sometimes party to other 'knowing' factors.

One lunch time Chocker, as usual, donned his coat, folded his Daily Mirror and announced he was off to the 'German cruiser' (boozer). This visit would inevitably take in the local bookies. Although he was a Brummie through and through he would often lapse into his own rhyming slang. The statement was also an invitation to all who were gathered and wished to frequent The Hazelwell pub with him.

Sir Stafford raised an eyebrow and casually looked over his broad rimmed glasses, but said nothing. Via the Birmingham Post, I had studied the race card for that evening's greyhounds at Kings Heath and had given the benefit of my wisdom, for all who were willing to listen, for one particular race. Chocker had, I thought, paid scant regard when I had expressed an opinion that Traps 1 and 3 would fill the first two places in the first race. In fact no one had shown any interest at all.

My forecast turned out to be correct and my 4s. (20p) yielded £3. 2s. (£3.10p), which incidentally was approximately 25% of a painter's wages at that time. Chocker had taken my advice and I became his friend for life, albeit a short one for him! I suppose Chocker's early demise would have been forecast as easily by me as the result of the 7.30 pm race at Kings Heath. He developed severe diabetes, but didn't curb his drinking and suffered gangrene to his right foot after sustaining a small cut when treading on a broken bottle. Amputation was quickly and almost inevitably followed by his death.

I attended his funeral, a strange diversity of mourners whose groupings, despite the occasion, displayed outward but unspoken hostility to one another. It was the consequence of his life style, one that was all too apparent, and hardly hidden from those who had merely a passing acquaintance with the now deceased Chocker.

A small group of his former colleagues stood, rather uncomfortably, between the factions at the graveside, dividing our condolences between both parties. His grave was on the boundary of the cemetery, an eight foot high, green metal palisade fence separated his resting place from a main road and shopping area.

"An ideal location," remarked one of my colleagues.

"Why's that?" I asked.

"Well, look there is a Bookies opposite and a pub fifty yards away."

"Yes, you are right, he will definitely be happy here."

Sir Stafford had, by this time, already gone. He was quite a bit older than his brothers but lived an idyllic, though childless, life with his lovely wife in a pre-war council house, situated in a small close in Harborne. It was a close I knew well, mainly because at its access was a bus stop which serviced buses I used on a regular basis. Indeed, I had sometimes met Sir Stafford at that very spot. There were few houses in the close, no more than ten, and everyone knew their neighbours and kept their eyes open for their welfare and wellbeing. The close was spotless, the houses were well maintained by the occupants and the gardens a mass of colour in the spring and summer.

Then Sir Stafford's elderly single neighbour died and, at that time, the City Council felt the need to pay due reverence to the radical ideology of amateurish social reformers. One such policy was to locate 'problem families' into established and settled communities, the theory being that their standards of living would rub off and rise to those of their new neighbours.

It was a disastrous edict for many communities and for the tolerant Sir Stafford, his wife and the rest of their little close it was an unmitigated failure. The 'problem family' were next door and for those in the close this one misplaced family became a nightmare from which, I firmly believe, Sir Stafford never really recovered. He told me of the six months of torment he and his wife suffered, the vandalisation of a nice house and the ruination of idyllic lives took its inevitable toll on Sir Stafford and his wife.

As a footnote, when the family were eventually evicted not a door remained and the new kitchen units had gone. Every length of copper pipe had been removed and a hitherto lovely garden had become a rubbish tip and dump. I have forever after had a grave mistrust of such inane doctrines and of those who pay credence to them and so would, I know, Sir Stafford.

30

And Along Came Another Dave!

With three years left of my apprenticeship along came another Dave. This one was short, stocky and bespectacled. No flat cap though for he was of the next generation of craftsmen and in many ways a breath of fresh air. He was, in fact, just five years older than I but no lesser craftsman than my mentors and better than some. His craftsmanship was soon recognised and he was immediately targeted for some very decent work. He was very much his own man, and his more up to date approach to virtually every aspect of our trade was at odds with some of my more elder mentors. However, no-one could argue that the end result was less than could be expected of an excellent craftsman.

'Young' Dave, as he was quickly to be known, had a wicked sense of humour, was nearly always in fine form and would lift spirits on the gloomiest of days, although a hangover would retard the process. This was a factor that often blighted the initial hours of his working day, but not his aptitude for the job he was engaged on. Young Dave loved his darts and, in all honesty, wasn't a bad player and the pub he played for, The Vine at Harborne, was a lovely little watering hole, which I sometimes frequented myself in later years. He though, was very much a 'regular' and, although you may have walked into the bar with him, you were soon unwittingly embroiled with a whole host of other regulars and acquaintances. A walk along

Harborne High Street with Dave always took twice as long as it should, for it was amazing just how many people he knew and wanted to chat to. Apart from darts, he was also in The Vine's bowls team and loved a game of golf with other interested regulars. Another reason why I often found myself with Young Dave as my mentor was that, like myself, he resided in Weoley Castle, albeit on the opposite side of the estate. He also had transport, an Austin A35 van, which gave him independence and a certain amount of freedom which no other 'chippie' on the section could aspire to. It suited Young Dave admirably and, it had to be said, he exploited the scenario but his work was always his priority. Some of the more staid and traditional resented certain features in the way his work was carried out, but never the ultimate quality.

Young Dave would often carry materials in his van; something management were quick to realise was highly beneficial to the department. Some of his colleagues felt he, and therefore them, were being taken advantage of and such activities needed proper ratification and enhanced payments. Their protestations were short lived however, but as I knew too well, Young Dave gained full recompense, not in monetary terms, but in the freedom and very flexible working times created by that freedom. He would often call and pick me up in the morning when we were working together. His aim was always to finish work at a 'reasonable hour'. I soon found this could be any time after 1.00 pm provided, of course, our work was completed. He always had work in hand somewhere in our 'theatre of operations' and that meant he was almost impossible to find, even if you wanted to, thus his illusiveness gained him the nickname of 'pimpernel'. He was a hard task master, good mentor, fun and an adventure was never far away.

The Man on the Moon is a large imposing public house, on a prominent corner location in the West Heath district of the city. It was once called The Man in the Moon until Neil Armstrong's epic and dramatic first steps onto the moon's surface and overnight a subtle name change was effected. Young Dave and I were working in a small sub-station opposite the pub, it was a bitterly cold day, a smoky grey sky fulfilled the promise of persistent flurries of snow. Our only source of heat was the sub-station transformer and we had taken our morning break huddled into its pulsating fins, the steam from our mugs of tea causing Dave's spectacle lenses to mist and setting my nose running. It was all very uncomfortable and we cracked on with our work to finish at lunchtime. Dave looked across the road to the welcoming lights emanating from the pub.

"Come on, let's go and get some warmth."

We packed away our gear into Dave's van and hurried through a gathering blizzard into a more than expected populated bar. Our fellow building workers on a nearby site had also given up the ghost and headed for the sanctuary of the Moon.

Dave went to the bar whilst I managed to gain a table and seats in close proximity to the dart board. It was not long before impromptu games of darts commenced which Dave watched intently as we ate our sandwiches, thawed out and went on to our second pint. Most of the players were from the adjacent building site and I sensed that Dave was getting itchy fingers. I was proved correct when Dave produced, like a rabbit from a magician's hat, a set of well-used and well-loved darts from his lunch box.

"Be prepared!" he said.

"Prepared for what?" I replied.

"A game of darts, don't let me down."

Darts were not my game, I excelled rarely and then only with luck. I had often played Dave and never won a game, this continual lack of success had left me dispirited, disinterested and convinced me that the only person I would be capable of beating would also be leaning on a white stick! I looked at Young Dave with apprehension.

"They're playing for pints and I haven't got that kind of money," I said.

Young Dave downed the rest of his pint. "You had better be on form then, lad," he retorted. The next thing I knew I was on the oche having very tentative practise throws at a dart board that looked far too small and very far away!

I think I remember our first 'best of three' against two convivial but oversized Irishmen. They were drinking pints of Guinness which was far dearer than our mild; this spurred me to greater concentration and endeavour. Thanks to Dave we won and two further pints of mild arrived at our table. Suddenly Young Dave was eliciting challengers, all of which were despatched. The dart board appeared to expand in size and my arrows screamed through the fog of cigarette smoke, honing in on their target with the dexterity of a world champion. I was elated and I was pissed. We had somehow exhausted challengers, had been offered a place in the pub's darts team and had a table full of mild ale, which we could not/dare not imbibe! How Dave drove home, in very dodgy road conditions, I don't know for I fell asleep. I woke up when Dave pushed me out of his van outside my home. His parting words were:

"Make sure you are up in the morning!"

I had no problem getting up next morning, but the hangover was something else!

The sixties and early seventies saw the city council embark on a massive programme of clearance of sub-standard housing in inner city areas and the creation of major housing estates at Castle Vale, Bromford, Druids Heath, Hawkesley, Chelmsley Wood, Frankley and smaller developments on brown field sites. Many of the high rise blocks of flats on Castle Vale, Bromford and Chelmsley Wood had sub-stations on their ground floors.

Each sub-station had two pairs of doors and one single panic or escape door. The design, which was a standard one, had been determined by the MEB's own architects department. They had determined that all doors should be fully ventilated, which meant that the doors were literally a framework of timbers with louver panel infills. The aim was to prevent the transformer from overheating. The design turned out to be an unwelcome facet, for the sub-stations where such doors were fitted became extremely dusty and the target of vandals who took delight in pushing a variety of inflammable items through the door louvers. The aim, of course, was to cause a fire, a prospect hardly welcome in a high rise block of flats! A panic stricken council and a culpable MEB thought it best that the louvers should be covered. The overheating of a transformer suddenly became a secondary consideration.

As a consequence the remedy of preventing such arson attacks was to clad the interior of the doors with asbestos panels and Young Dave and I were nominated for the job, mainly because of Dave's independent mobility via his A35 van. Three 8' x 4' asbestos sheets were delivered to all affected tower block sub-stations. Young Dave was given a list of locations and a free hand in how, or by what order, the work was done. This of course suited my mentor because it was obvious that the spread of the work would make us almost impossible to find.

We did not know, nobody knew, of the long term health issues of us working with the potentially highly dangerous asbestos. And so we cut the sheets by hand, drilled them for screw fixing and sanded the edges. It was, of course, not the only time that we had worked with the material, for it was in general use for a variety of fire protection and insulation work as well as for lagging. The long term effects are surfacing in an ever increasing number of workers across the industrial spectrum, inheriting its deadly consequences.

It was midday at Harborne Church Farm golf course on a normal working day that I stood taking a variety of practise swings on the first tee, copying the professionals I had seen on television. I had never played golf before but my mentor had arranged a foursome with two Austin night workers who were regulars at The Vine. Young Dave had rushed us through our day's quota of sub-stations to make the date. I could do no more that be with him. The other two had a full complement of very impressive golfing gear. Bags of clubs, trolleys, balls, tees, golf shoes and garish harlequin patterned jumpers. I had removed my overalls, Dave had hired my clubs and had given me four balls and four tees, winked a sly wink under a broad checked cap and whispered: "Don't let me down!" The other three drove off with variable efficiency, it was now my turn. I swung the club selected for me by Dave and miss after miss ensued and I just kept swinging. My playing partners moved off in the direction of the first green, either through embarrassment of my abortive attempts, or thinking that at my current rate of progress, darkness would fall, our round uncompleted.

I was already to miss out the first hole when a less than sympathetic voice from a following group of players bellowed:

"Keep your bloody eye on the ball lad!"

I did as he said and swung, eureka! Contact made, the ball fair flew on and on, veered to the left and cleared the wall surrounding the graveyard of St. Peter's parish church. Applause ensued from behind me and elated I turned to milk it. The same know-all told me I had 'gone out of bounds'. Not quite knowing in golf terms the implications, I moved off at a spritely pace to where I thought the ball would be, I clambered over the churchyard wall and searched for what seemed to be an eternity and found my missile, nesting in gravel, twixt a vase of flowers and a granite headstone. The depleted foursome were now miles away, having given up on my feeble efforts and lack of nous. I wandered back dejectedly to the pro-shop and handed in my hired clubs and enjoyed a free cup of tea with the assistant professional.

Dave never asked me to play golf again and I had no inclination to do so. He hardly spoke to me at all next day, there was no rollicking though because he knew and I knew that being on a golf course in the noon day sun was not in the script for that working day – or any working day!

31

Asbestos Dust Rained Down On Everyone, Shop Staff, Customers And Us!

The MEB flag ship shop/showroom in the city centre in 1959 was situated in Paradise Street. It was located on the ground floor of a large late Victorian building, very similar to so many in the city at that time, darkened, detracted and eroded of its former splendour. Next door was the gas showroom, pre-nationalisation of course, the city owned both its electric and gas supply departments.

I worked at Paradise Street on a number of occasions but, with the coming of redevelopment in that area of the city, it meant that any work we carried out was purely to see the shop through to its imminent closure. What used to fascinate me was the small workshop at the rear of the shop where a couple of electricians would repair kettles, irons and numerous other small electrical appliances in apparent organised chaos. Many customers could wait for a diagnosis, prognosis, costing and a very speedy repair if warranted. That was the service that was available in those days, and it was a service for which MEB staff at Paradise Street were justifiably proud. We always appreciated our lunch time with the electricians, tea provided and the chance of a good chat.

As a consequence of that unfailing service, there was nearly always a formidable queue both in and outside the shop, for it was also a pay point for electricity bills. I was working in the shop one day when such a queue had formed. A gentleman, who had waited patiently, eventually reached the counter to pay his bill only to be told it was his gas bill, and he was directed next door to the gas showroom. Having cursed his own stupidity and apologised to the cashier, he left the shop – via the plate glass window! To everyone's amazement, he was completely unharmed and carried on without further word to the gas board shop next door.

When closure eventually came, a suitable replacement site was found in a new building at the junction of New Street and Ethel Street. Due to the decline in gradient of Ethel Street from New Street the shop had two floors, was in a prime location, in a street with one of the highest real estate values in Europe. It was the flag ship outlet of MEB shops and compared to Paradise Street reflected the new image of commercial retail shopping that was integral to a newly developed city centre. Gone was the individuality of Paradise Street, its persona of the forties, its preoccupation for public service and the now outdated principles of 'the consumer comes first'. The shop was all about profit, profit at all cost. Because of the location and the enormous overheads it incurred, profit targets were hardly ever achieved but that didn't seem to matter, MEB had a prime location in one of the busiest retail streets, certainly in Britain at least. Unfortunately the repairs workshop and its two electricians had no place in this format of commercial enterprise. A new city, a new dawn and a chance to disassociate itself from one of the essential principles of nationalisation – public service. The layout of the New Street shop reflected its purely commercial perspective, for the payment counter for electricity accounts, which was by far the main reason for people setting foot into its portals, was situated on the basement floor. So, to pay your electric bill you first had to walk through a ground floor, full of electrical appliances and enterprising staff, descend a staircase and walk through more appliances and preying staff to a counter situated at the furthest point from the stairs. There were two pay points at the counter and the queues were often as long as those at the old Paradise Street shop.

It soon became clear that, although the general public would happily pay their accounts at New Street, their enthusiasm to purchase items of electrical equipment was a different matter. The two car park spaces for the shop manager and his deputy were priced at £600 a month each, thus the car park spaces were eventually reduced to one and then the manager's space suffered a similar fate in an attempt to make a profit, or at least to balance the books. It was not long before a major revamp of the basement area was to take place. The fact of the matter was that the original lighting was just not adequate enough and descending from an exceedingly bright and dynamic ground floor to a dull and claustrophobic basement did little to encourage potential customers to open wallets and purses.

The upgrade in lighting involved significant alterations to the suspended, false ceiling. New lighting units fitted, the suspended ceiling had to be rearranged around them. The work fell to Young Dave and I, the work involved was extensive and not easy for hardly any of the original ceiling tiles fitted and, in the new found spirit of frugality, as few as possible new tiles were to be used. We set about our task readily, cutting and refitting tiles as required over a period of four days, by which time the work was completed.

Ten years later and that work would not have been allowed to take place, for the tiles were made of asbestos! No-one truly knew the dangers of the material in those days, but at times the basement area resembled a fog as asbestos dust rained down on everyone, shop staff, customers and ourselves! It was impossible to know how many people were affected by their co-incidental presence in the shop over those days. I have often wondered how many people died not knowing how they had succumbed to a truly dreadful and deadly disease by simply standing in a queue waiting to pay their electricity account. Fifty years on people could still be wondering why and how. We did not know that we would be party to their potential demise, nor did we have reason to consider the danger to our MEB colleagues or its future effect on us. It is a legacy that I must live with, although because of the wide scale use of asbestos related products, and MEB used plenty of them, it can only be considered a contributory factor that I happened to work on this particular task at the New Street shop at that time.

The haunting fact that the simple task of sawing or drilling an asbestos tile, and its possible effect on the lives of ordinary people many years on, is something that sometimes wakens me in the small hours.

32

A Death At The Bulls Head

Midlands Electricity Board, who had for some time been very proactive in pursuing retail outlets known as showrooms, chose a new development at Auchinleck Square, Five Ways, to increase its portfolio of shops in the Birmingham area. It is quite surprising to note that MEB had between thirty and thirty-five shops at the time in the Birmingham area alone. I, along with two mentors, were despatched to fit out our new acquisition. The shop was situated at the southern entrance to the square and was one of the larger units on the site.

It was cold, very cold, and that entrance to the square which was from Tennant Street and its junction with Islington Row, formed a perfect wind tunnel that an unglazed unit and flimsy hoarding failed to minimize. The maxim, of course, in those now far off days was that you worked to keep warm. So, when lunchtime arrived we decamped to the local hostelry, The Bull's Head which was on the corner of Tennant Street and Bishopgate Street. It was a nice little pub and the landlord had no problem with us consuming our own sandwiches. There were normally no more than five or six in the bar, so we three, with six pints of mild between us, accounted for much of his business. Above all it was warm and cosy and a real drag to leave.

Our drinking companions in the small bar were nearly always the same, a nice old lady and her son, and a patron who seemed to spend the whole of our half hour with the Sporting Life spread before him, studying form intensely and knocking back pints for inspiration. We were two weeks into the job, thoroughly enjoying the demands of the work for our showrooms were always palatially fitted, and also enjoying our new compulsive love affair with the warmth of The Bulls Head.

This particular day we entered the bar and acknowledged our greetings from the landlord and our usual lunchtime companions and resumed the usual seats, each with our pints of mild and sandwiches set out on the bar tables before us. The old lady, as usual, was seated to my left, I set about my corned beef sandwiches, a particular favourite of mine, and my two mentors to my right were also relishing the comfort and hospitality. It was therefore something of a shock when I received a sudden nudge in the rib from Dave's elbow, my workmate on my immediate right, just as I was about to attack my second sandwich.

"The old lady's just died," he remarked.

I looked at Dave, waiting for a punch line which didn't come. Still open mouthed, I turned my head to the left to see the old lady, chin on chest, headscarf askew, and her hand still holding the remains of her half-pint on the table before her. Liverpool Jim, my other mentor, a devoted Roman Catholic, there are none more devout than from that city, was frantically crossing himself, his lips betraying a sombre unheard prayer. I looked towards the old lady's son who was gazing out of the window into the street as if in a trance, shedding no tears or showing any recognition, totally oblivious to what had just occurred. Dave called the landlord; we finished our drinks, wrapped the remains of our lunch and, together with Sporting Life man, offered our condolences to the still hypnotised son, and left.

We walked slowly up Tennant Street, it was the first time I had witnessed death.

"How did you know she had died Dave?" I asked.

"I heard the rattle son, the rattle of death!" he replied.

Liverpool Jim nodded, crossed himself again but said nothing. The happening, of course, did not put an end to our lunchtime visits to The Bull's Head. We went in on the day of the old lady's funeral, when on the bar was the most wonderful floral tribute, a vacant chair of exquisite beauty. I have witnessed death a few times since that day and none has been comparable to the peace and tranquillity of that lady's passing. A shock yes, for all of us and probably her one regret would have been that her time elapsed before her chance to finish her half pint of beer!

At that time it was normal to receive our weekly wages, wherever practical, on the site on which we worked. Due to our permanency over several weeks, our wage packets would arrive on a Friday morning via two wages clerks who would tour such sites in one of the MEB pool cars, the wages being carried in a wooden varnished carrying case. One Friday after opening and checking my pay packet, and contemplating for a moment what I could do with my 'vast' disposal income, I noticed that Dave was sitting on a saw bench, leaning forward with flat cap pushed back far enough to expose his grey, thinning hair, and in deep thought, perusing his pay slip.

"You alright Dave?" I asked with some concern. Eventually he replied.

"Yes son, you know if you had told me forty years ago that I would be earning nearly £800 a year in my lifetime I would have said you were off your head!" How times have changed.

Eventually we successfully concluded with some pride our work in Auchinleck Square. Sadly I never did enjoy the hospitality of The Bull's Head again, old Dave and Liverpool Jim are long since gone but over the years we often recalled that particular job, more for the passing of a very nice old lady, than for any other. That lunchtime, The Bull's Head and Tennant Street will be forever with me, together with my eternal love of corned beef sandwiches.

33

For Queen, Country, MEB – And Reg!

Redundancy after thirty years' service to one company was a terrible shock for Frank. Certainly there was not a more conscientious, friendly, industrious, generous and sober of gentlemen. Apparently there was little warning that his services to the Metropolitan Cammel and Carriage Company were no longer required. His age would have certainly been against him if, in the very doubtful scenario, that a job for a carriage fitter was ever to become available in the foreseeable future. The poor chap must have envisaged his future wealth and security with some apprehension.

Redemption for Frank came in the form of his brother, who worked at Nechells Power Station, for the Central Electricity Generating Board. He had been casually scanning a notice board on which were pinned internal situations vacant within the electricity supply industry and had noted that MEB Birmingham was requiring a carpenter and joiner.

As mentioned previously 'a pull' within the industry was a major asset when such situations did become vacant. There is in fact a world of difference between the work of a skilled carriage fitter and that of a carpenter. That divide is much closer however when it comes to joinery work – especially that in a joinery workshop. An extra glowing reference from his former employer, his stability in his employment in the past and his amenable character made Frank an excellent choice.

He accepted that he would be on a new learning curve, with much of the work he had to do but, as we all found out quickly, Frank was a very fast learner and not afraid to ask if in any doubt. That won him a great deal of respect from my mentors. Everything Frank did was first-class and, in time, he became more and more adept and less reliant on others.

Although Frank had never been in a ring, his features resembled those of a boxer. He had thinning sandy hair which was gradually succumbing to greyness, a rather flat nose, puffy eyes behind thick rimmed spectacles and a sallow roundness to his face. Unusually for operatives of our building section he was strictly teetotal which gained him some ribbing, but also a reluctant respect. Whenever we sought lunchtime comfort in a hostelry, Frank would be quite happy to join us, partaking of a lemonade or orange juice and always insisting that he paid his turn, despite our protestations.

Having spent the past thirty odd years in a claustrophobic factory he knew little of the world beyond his former employment at Washwood Heath, Castle Bromwich where his wartime had been spent producing Spitfire Fighters and Lancaster Bombers and his home in Erdington. He relished more than most his exploring of Birmingham via his work placements. He was like a boy ticking the numbers in a book with the sight of a newly seen locomotive, for Frank was seeing districts of the city he had only ever heard of via the Birmingham Evening Mail or the Evening Dispatch. So, in the end, he found his employment adventurous, interesting and rewarding.

One of Frank's work placements was Dale End which, no doubt Reg considered would ease him in gently. It was here that he commenced a long running friendship with Old Dave with whom he shared an interest in crosswords. Frank would bring in his Sunday Observer and he and Dave would toil their lunch breaks to fully complete the crossword before the next edition. One day Reg turned up for his afternoon cup of tea in a more urgent and agitated state than usual. His red face glowed and beads of sweat trickled down his forehead. I grabbed his cup and poured him his tea.

"Did you know that the Queen is driving up Dale End tomorrow?" he enquired.

Dave stirred from his thoughts. "I wondered why the flags were out," he sarcastically remarked. Reg ignored or perhaps didn't detect the sarcasm in Dave's comment. He adopted his typical pose when about to partake of his afternoon cuppa. We all watched with anticipation as he gently raised HIS bone china cup, little finger delicately hooked from its handle, blinking like a rabbit in a car's headlights, as he took his first sip. Every sip was a carbon copy of the first, just like the very proper routine of a lady who had attended a posh finishing school. Afternoon tea at Dale End was a world away from Claridges, but for Reg's etiquette.

Reg, however, was contemplative.

"The route was in the Mail last night," I helpfully added.

Reg disregarded my remark. "His nibs wants bunting up on the frontage, says we are the only buildings in the city without, where the hell am I supposed to get bunting at this juncture?"

If there is one thing that my mentors were adept at, it was sensing just the slightest whiff of overtime. It was 3.00 pm and 'his nibs' wanted bunting on our Dale End frontage by the morning. Unseen by Reg, Dennis winked at Dave.

"Leave it with us Reg I might be able to lay my hands on some, no promises at this short hour though."

Even I noticed an air of confidence in Dennis' tone.

As soon as Reg had departed the carpenters shop to make his way back to Piers Road, Dennis left us too. Dave reckoned that Dennis knew the whereabouts of some bunting and that we would be working over as we would have to drape it via the large windows of the offices, which we would not be allowed to do whilst office staff were at work. Dennis returned with four sacks full of bunting, apparently left over from the Coronation, and waited until 4.30 pm before ringing Reg, who by that time would have sanctioned all night working to get him off the hook! Thus that night we worked through 'till 7.00 pm, festooning our office frontages with ancient, but highly decorative flags of red, white and blue. We hung out of windows, used boxes of drawing pins and rolls of tape, and when we had finished the MEB offices looked a treat. An early visit from Reg next morning brought a huge smile to his face. He instructed us to remove the decorations after hours that night, another bonus. So pleased was he, no question was raised as to where Dennis requisition bunting from, he was just grateful that he would be lauded for his efforts.

There was however an interesting sequel to our overtime. For thirty years Frank had beaten a path, in his former life, from Washwood Heath to his Erdington home, arriving at virtually the same time every evening. On the night of the 'bunting' Frank didn't arrive home until 7.30 pm. By that time his panic stricken wife and daughter had contacted the local hospitals and also telephoned the police! Frank was livid, but I suppose that the actions of his family were probably understandable. When told we would be working over to take down our glorious decorations, he telephoned his neighbour to tell his wife that he would be late home again. We had to explain to Frank that short notice overtime was often a feature with our work which was sometimes responsive to potential dangers to the public. Bunting removed and stowed away, wherever Dennis had hidden it, it was never to see another royal celebration.

Frank worked his time 'till his retirement at 65 with MEB. With some three years to go arthritis in his hands gradually became worse and meant that he could no longer handle tools which made all of us very sad. MEB was an excellent employer and Frank a loyal and respected employee, so he ended his service working in the Summer Lane stores. Despite his ailments, a comparatively happy end to his working life for our much esteemed colleague.

34

"Keep A Knockin', But You Can't Come In"

A Song Recorded By Little Richard In 1957

Any instructions that Reg gave regarding one of his jobs always included chapter and verse and minute detail on how on reach our destination. This was, of course, the A-Z of Birmingham as interpreted by our foreman and which involved as little bus travel as possible. Bus travel meant the issue of plastic tokens and thereby the plundering of the petty cash tin, the frugal Reg was adverse to throwing MEB money around like confetti, his frugality did not, however, extend to our shoe leather or our personal fitness. There were just three basic rules. You could walk as far as you like (as long as it didn't impinge on any work schedule), corporation bus travel was to be minimized, and Midland Red usage was taboo within the city boundaries (travel by Midland Red, within the city boundaries, was more expensive than by corporation transport). Any of the above options meant apprentices sagging at the knees under the weight of a bag of tools and my more elderly mentors seeking resuscitation every ten minutes via a Woodbine.

One day, Reg was in a happy mood for he was imparting to Hubert, my mentor, that we were working at the sub-station in the grounds of All Saints Hospital in Winson Green only a mile away, no bus just a brisk and invigorating stroll from Piers Road. Hubert was a comparative newcomer but was a fast learner and, having fallen foul of one of Reg's route marches, now listened with a deadpan expression and an occasional glance in my direction as Reg dissected every paving slab, cobble and kerb of our route. Reg departed and Hubert turned to me;

"Do you know where we are going?" I nodded. "Good," he said, "'cos I haven't got a clue!" Just six months earlier Hubert has been plying his craft in his native Jamaica!

We wended our way through the streets of Hockley and Winson Green, me carrying the tools and lunch, Hubert with two lengths of timber of his shoulder. After half an hour we arrived at the gates of All Saints Mental Hospital. A high wall surrounded its grounds and it had, as its very close neighbour, Winson Green Prison. The sub-station was within the grounds, backing onto the boundary wall and opposite the hospital kitchen. Our various jobs would run into the next day when I would be at college and Reg had arranged for another apprentice, just a bit younger than me, to replace me.

Not long after commencing our work we had the company of Dusty, one of the sub-station attendants for that part of the city. Dusty was well past the now retirement age and looked something like the cartoon character Mr. Magoo. Thickened lenses in his spectacles bore testament to his very poor eyesight. He was a man of few words and was very sprightly for his years. His task was to clean the sub-station and its gear and enter his works into the sub-station log book, together with the various readings he had to take. All the sub-station attendants were either of very little conversation or that chatty you could not shut them up. We always thought it was their job that made them this way inclined for they nearly always worked on their own and could go all day travelling from sub-station to sub-station without seeing another employee. Dusty was of the former species!

Dusty was busying himself inside the sub-station whilst Hubert and I tackled some external work. Behind us was the sound of much chattering and laughter and we both turned around to see a group of about twelve women of various ages walking towards us. The walk became a jog and it was obvious we were their target. We glanced at each other, grabbed the tools and ran round to the sub-station frontage only to find that a panic stricken Dusty had locked himself inside. We hammered on the doors, pleading to Dusty to let us in, but to no avail as Dusty was not going to let down the drawbridge to his workmates. We turned to face the obviously deranged women who had formed a semi-circle in front of us, our backs against the sub-station doors. We were then the butt of various lewd comments and suggestions which we were just about able to treat with nervous good humour.

Hubert continuing to tap the door with a hammer held at his side, in the vain hope that Dusty would relent. We were in a predicament and could not believe the group were not attended. Help came in the guise of a man in white coat, yes literally, on a bicycle. We heard him shouting some way off but could not make out what he was trying to relay until he was almost with us. "Don't give them matches, don't give them matches," he kept shouting. There was no chance of that as neither myself nor Hubert smoked, Dusty did though, but he was safely ensconced witnessing the siege by peeping through the sub-station door louvers. The 'White Coat' jumped from his bike, "Come on now ladies, leave the gentlemen alone and come and have your lunches." The ladies began dispersing and headed across the road to the hospital kitchen and canteen. We stood shell shocked. The 'White Coat' gave his apologies and asked again if we had handed out matches, reassured by us, he shepherded his flock through the canteen doors. We breathed a sigh of relief. Then the shaky voice of Dusty was heard within his stronghold, "Have they gone?"

"Yes Dusty, but we told them that you were the only one who smoked and that they should come back later and you would give them a box of Swan," I replied.

"Bloody hell, you didn't, did you?" There was much rushing around within the sub-station as Dusty upped considerably his leisurely pace to complete his duties. Half an hour later Dusty poked his head around a cautiously opened door. "I'll be off then," he said. We laughed as he made the quickest exit he could, down the road towards the entrance gates and safety.

There were two very interesting sequels to those events, spaced quite a few years apart. As mentioned earlier I was at technical college the day after being taken hostage by the fairer sex, replaced by another apprentice just a bit younger than I. Hubert needed boiling water for a cuppa and despatched the apprentice, with tea can, to the hospital kitchen. The lad was gone some time and Hubert was on the point of going to look for him when he saw my replacement running from the kitchen doors. It turned out that he too had to contend with some very close attention by female kitchen workers, who had locked him in a vegetable store. He refused point blank to revisit the scene and offered to buy Hubert's tea at a nearby café. That same apprentice, just a few years after, gave up his craft to convey the word of God, according to his sect, in a full-time capacity. I often wonder if his experience at All Saints had any bearing on his career change.

Some five years later, in the midst of my long but unspectacular junior football career, I had a couple of years playing for a team who played in the same league system as the staff team from All Saints. They had their own pitch within the hospital grounds and we happened to draw them in a cup competition at the hospital. It was a closely fought game with considerable home support on the touch lines. Very late on in the game the referee awarded us a rather dubious penalty kick from which we scored to win the game 1-0. There was a great deal of hostility and abuse from the disgruntled home supporters. When we got back to the sanctuary of the changing rooms we found that much of our clothing had been purloined. We complained and eventually our clothes were returned to us in a wheel barrow. It had apparently happened before, the culprit being an over enthusiastic supporter of the hospital football team and an inmate!

35

"There Is No Good In Arguing With The Inevitable – The Only Argument Available With An East Wind Is To Put On Your Overcoat"

Democracy and Address

By the end of my apprenticeship I could boast, with some pride, that I had accomplished the feat of travelling on every Birmingham City Transport bus route of the mid-Sixties. What made this achievement more remarkable was that it was done without the specific aim in mind, purely by journeys to and from a multiplicity of work sites. If Reg had more input into this epic I would have never reached this goal for most of my travel would have been on foot!

Today, in an age when the family car is as much a part of life as our daily bread, those bus journeys wouldn't rate entry on any job application. They may have been a help in those distant days, for knowledge of the city and its suburbs were a useful asset to have then in a variety of jobs. I must admit now, apart from my own local buses, I haven't a clue which routes buses take to reach their ultimate destination. Deregulation of bus services in the 80s meant many other bus companies came to the city and local services, for the first time, were able to extend their routes beyond city boundaries and nothing was quite the same again.

Harry and I had walked down the Chester Road, Castle Bromwich from our sub-station site near Timberley Lane.

Harry was not in the most amiable mood which was unusual for him and he was less so when he felt the city's bus services were contriving against him. We stood at the terminus at the Clock Garage, Harry checking his pocket watch at regular intervals. He was a stickler for punctuality, a trait I suspect that Reg found infuriating, for he would have found satisfaction in hauling him over the coals for violation of the good time-keeping code. Reg had long given up hope of any indiscretion by Harry in that respect. In truth out wait was not a particularly long one but I could see Harry was becoming more and more agitated as time elapsed.

We boarded the bus and sat on the lower deck. Harry's expectation that our departure was imminent was dashed when the conductor produced a tea can and cups, he and his driver lit cigarettes and they stood around the terminus clock for what seemed an age. Harry's usually long fuse finally blew. He rose from his seat at my side and without a word walked back down the bus with the obvious aim of confronting the conductor and driver. I cringed and self-consciously looked back towards where Harry's tirade was emanating. My workmate was a chatterer even when he wasn't upset but when he adopted his angry pose, thumbs in waistcoat pockets, cap pulled forward which accentuated further his pointed features, he became the engine that drove an unstoppable vitriolic diatribe. I had seen that phenomenon before and other participants wilted to dumbness as each gave us any attempt to intercede. The driver and conductor were no exceptions. Harry, finally exhausted, his expression of exasperation. The stunned silence of both men was broken with a surprisingly calm and level headed explanation by the driver of just why he could not move his vehicle before its allotted time slot and, having only just left Washwood Heath bus garage, he had no idea what had happened to the bus that should have departed fifteen minutes before his.

Harry returned muttering to his seat and I hoped that the matter was finished as we started our journey. The conductor, however, had recovered from Harry's verbal onslaught and it was very obvious from his sullen demeanour that he would not let Harry off without giving an adequate response. After a short while he arrived at our side, "Fares," he said, in a tone which indeed spoke volumes.

"Town," I said. He plucked the money from my hand and all but threw the ticket back."Fares," he said again. Harry bit straight, "Fox and Goose."

"Fox and Goose!" exclaimed the clippie, "all that fuss for five stops?" in a tone that could be interpreted as sarcastic.

Harry ignored the comment but I just knew he would have his pound of flesh before he left the scene at the Fox and Goose. Harry was swiftly out of his seat after the penultimate stop before his. He put a consoling hand on my shoulder, "See you tomorrow son," he said in farewell.

The expected furore started immediately Harry arrived on the platform of the bus where his recently acquired arch enemy was standing in anticipation of what was to come. Harry had already told me not to get involved and I happily complied, shrinking even lower in my seat, but not enough not to see what was going on.

The argument was in full swing as the bus reached the stop opposite the Fox and Goose, which was Harry's drop off point. Harry and the conductor were still trading insults as the conductor followed Harry off the platform. A melee ensued as oncoming passengers became entangled with the main protagonists around the stop. Things began to get out of hand even further when the increasingly antagonistic conductor had to contend, not only with the very rapid spat of my mentor, but also a bluff, rotund man who was less than pleased with a half-hour wait for his transport. He too was becoming frustrated with his lack of input into the continuing mud-slinging of Harry and the conductor. The bus remained stationary and some passengers were wondering when movement might commence and some began shouting that we really should be on our way.

The calming influence of the driver eventually appeared just as his overwhelmed colleague was about to swing his ticket machine at Harry and the interfering fat man. An elderly lady shouted to the driver to fetch an inspector, Harry turned to the lady: "Madam, the only inspectors visible at this hour are located outside Fort Dunlop, one outside Joseph Lucas in Great King Street, one outside the Austin at Longbridge and one chained to a lamppost at Bournville!" that was a reference to Cadbury's.

"You're a clever sod you are," said the conductor being held back by the driver.

"He is," said the fat man.

"Can we go driver?" was the general call from the passengers.

The conductor turned to fire a final salvo at Harry, but Harry had gone. He had indeed made his point. I craned my neck to see where Harry had got to and there he was, across the road, boarding an outer circle bus to Hall Green. I spent the rest of the journey looking out of the window and avoiding at all costs the glare of a ruffled conductor.

The City terminus arrived all too quickly and the clippie looked daggers at me as I walked towards the platform.

"Is that idiot likely to be catching this bus tomorrow?" he asked.

"No," I replied.

"Thank the Lord for that," he said. "I would have changed my shift."

Harry was a match for anyone in an argument! It was a very short but very eventful journey – the result of a missing scheduled bus, an irate Harry who wished to get home as soon as possible to an ailing wife and an aggressive conductor who would not let the matter rest. It was for me, as a friend and fellow traveller, embarrassing and I was concerned for old Harry. Now, when I recall the scenario, I do so with a smile.

36

"Could You Tell Me How You Arrived At This Point?"

10th August, 1959 seemed an eternity away from 5th January, 1965, a remote notation on a distant calendar which I knew sometime, God willing, I would finally reach. The date was a significant one for it was the day I reached the age of twenty-one. My apprenticeship had finally concluded, my mentors had instilled into me as much practical wisdom as they possibly could and my college tutors had coaxed me through examinations and encouraged my thirst for knowledge. They were right of course, for you never ever complete your apprenticeship for there is always more to learn.

My new found status was tempered with trepidation. I would be on my own, no-one to lean on anymore, my decisions, all my own work and in life's great circle of work I would be passing my skills to another generation of carpenters and joiners. I should, however, have been facing the future confidently for in truth my foreman had anticipated my coming change of status by giving me more and more confidence building work over the last two years. Challenging carpentry and joinery work that required thought and nous. The adaption had been painless and virtually unnoticed, I was in fact fulfilling a craftsman's roll at ¾ and then ⅞ of a craftsman's pay. I was well aware of that fact but cared little of the monetary aspect. I was carrying out the tasks I enjoyed and hoping that my fellow craftsmen and great grandfather were looking down on my progress, proud that at least some of his genes had passed to me.

There was, suddenly, an air of secrecy and silence in the workplace, conversations were discontinued when I appeared, and there was whispering and nodding, nudging and asides. Something was going on but it was obvious that I was not to be involved. Of course, I had noticed, but I was far more concerned that, as 5th January approached, that I would have a call to meet the boss who would inform me that, despite my best efforts, my employment was no longer required. This was a common occurrence for the newly qualified apprentice in those times. That call, however, never came and the closer I came to my birthday the more secure and self-confident I became. I discovered on my birthday that the secrecy and subterfuge was indeed all about me.

A collection taken across the department has yielded a substantial amount, enough for a celebration buffet at a club where Liverpool Jim was a committee member that was located close to the city centre. The celebration was planned for 7th January, which, it appeared had already been much anticipated by both my mentors and fellow apprentices. The 5th arrived and was a strange mixture of normality and celebration. There were congratulations, the touching presentation of a prestigious Stabila Level by my colleagues, a certificate stating that I had satisfactorily completed my apprenticeship was presented by a senior engineer and then it was work as usual.

At lunchtime I bought a couple of rounds of drinks at our local, The Black Eagle, for those who were working in Piers Road. The main celebration, however, was to come. Liverpool Jim's social club was affiliated to the city's Roman Catholic

Cathedral of St. Chad's and was situated within a much larger building in Princip Street. I was picked up from my home and taxied to the event by Young Dave in his trusty work horse, the A35 Austin van. All my colleagues were ensconced and predictably slightly lubricated by my arrival. There were cheers as I entered the room and Old Dave thrust a pint into my hand:

"No concessions now lad, you are a fully blowed 'un, get this down you for starters."

It was a wondrous, real pub buffet and Liverpool Jim had pulled out all the stops. Huge pork pies, massive links of black pudding, wedges of Cheddar cheese, thick slices of ham, a vast array of sandwiches and a range of pickles. A dart board, snooker tables, cribbage, dominoes and discreet background music, Jim had thought of it all. The jewel in the crown, though, was a good pint of beer and as befits a predominately Irish club, a superb draught Guinness. The bar staff were very busy until well after official closing time.

When, eventually Liverpool Jim rang the bell for the final time, he had rung it several times prior to midnight, it really was time to give our thanks and say 'goodnight'. Young Dave offered a taxi service to his namesake, my brother and I – Hall Green, Cotteridge and Weoley Castle, quite a round trip and the driver would have certainly failed any police examination regarding alcohol intake. Young Dave, however, never gave any indication, outwardly, of just how much he had consumed.

We piled into the A35, Dave the elder and my brother in the rear seats, me in the passenger birth. We left Princip Street and took the turn into Corporation Street and had travelled just a short way when Dave had to swerve violently to avoid a man on a bicycle with a ladder on his shoulder, who came careering towards us in the middle of the road. Dave was about to exchange 'niceties' with the cyclist when he realised that our particular section of Corporation Street had been made one-way and not in our favour. A hint of panic ensued as Dave tried to address the situation with an immediate right turn, unfortunately also a one-way street!

Of all the streets in the city centre perhaps Newton Street is one of the most heavily policed. Next to the crown court and adjacent to Steelhouse Lane Police Station, it is at the very centre of the city's law enforcement complex. It was inevitable then that at the end of this narrow, short street were two torchlights indicating that we should stop, held by two police constables. The merriment and laughter in the rear passenger seats quickly subsided as realisation of our impending plight became clear to our inebriated travelling companions. Dave the elder sneezed twice violently, then belched which heralded a stream of Guinness from his nasal passages, the phenomenon causing stifled laughter from brother and former mentor.

A gaunt and serious Young Dave applied his handbrake, pleaded with the passengers to be quiet and before the policemen could move forward was out of the van and going to meet them. We sat silently, Old Dave busily and rather unsteadily wiping regurgitated Guinness from his coat and trousers. One torch had shone briefly over the occupants of the van, a long conversation ensued out of hearing, with Young Dave standing as steady as a rock as though, appropriately for the location, he was as sober as a judge. He returned to the van smiling,

"What happened I asked?"

"They wanted to know how I had arrived at this point, I told them I wasn't familiar with the one-way system and panicked. One reached for his notebook and I thought I was going to be done, then they asked where I had been, I told them. They looked at one another, the notebook went back in the pocket and they told me to park up somewhere and catch a bus home. All very strange," he said.

Young Dave parked up for about twenty minutes at our Summer Lane depot and when he thought the coast was clear we continued to our first drop at Hall Green by which time the jollity and merriment in the rear seats was no more, replaced by snoring and nodding heads and an occasional waft of Guinness. We arrived at Old Dave's Hall Green abode, which was located in a quiet cul-de-sac and, with as much dexterity as possible, in an attempt to maintain as much decorum and respect for Dave's neighbours. Our good intentions were, however, to be thwarted by the occupants of the rear seats, who when awakened decided to duet a chorus from The Desert Song.

Although we wished only Old Dave's departure, my brother also tried to vacate his seat as well. Curtains twitched as we managed to separate the noisy vocalists and point Dave in the direction of his garden gate. He staggered towards it humming an undetermined tune and for some unaccountable reason, apart from his inebriation, decided to ignore the logic of his gate and step over his garden wall. A fall followed and Dave lay prone in a border, laughing. We looked on in horror, our fast get away from the quiet, residential close was halted. Old Dave rose to his feet, turned and waved, and then made it safely to his porch door. We beat a hasty retreat through a guard of honour of faceless residents, peering into the darkness in an attempt to see the cause of their disturbance.

The next drop was Cotteridge where my brother and his wife lived with my uncle. I was hoping for a quick and quiet exit. Young Dave and I managed to extradite my brother from the van and, in view of Old Dave's demise, escorted him through the garden gate and propped him against his front door frame, rang the bill and quickly made our exit.

I knew eventually I must face my sister-in-law and she would be far from enamoured by the activities of husband and brother-in-law. Next day I managed to get to Piers Road on time but with very little time to spare. I entered the joiners shop and into a strangely silent atmosphere. Only one bench was occupied, the very end one. Old Dave was leaning forward, elbows on bench and head cradled in his hands, his cap pulled down and muffler encompassing his chin.

"That was a good night lad," he said.

I made a cup of tea and put it in front of him, he nodded his thanks. Dennis eventually paid his 'flock' a visit.

"What a night!" he said. "Any aspirin in the first-aid box?"

"No," said Dave, "I have had a look, just bandages and splints."

So my first job as a fully blown carpenter and joiner was a visit to the chemist for aspirins, just like old times! Work was at a premium that morning, at 12.30 Old Dave was slowly recovering.

"Time for a livener, are you coming?"

I knew Old Dave's remedy for hangovers well, and for him and me it worked. So, Old Dave and I engaged with the bar of The Black Eagle and knocked back a pint of mild with a bottle of Indian tonic water, added at intervals, as we drank down our glass. Just the one and then back to work.

Next morning Liverpool Jim breezed into Piers Road, he had wisely opted to take a day's holiday after his hard work organising my birthday celebrations and his extended hours behind the bar. All the participants in that joyous occasion were now recovered and fully in gear with their work mode.

At 9.30 am some months later at the end of my work bench stood a young lad with long hair, he wore new brown bib and brace overalls, stiff and starchy and straight from the stores. The lad bore a very apprehensive countenance.

"What can I do for you?" I asked.

"I am the new apprentice, Jim," he answered. "I was told to report to Mr. Betteridge for instruction."

"Really, well my first instruction to you young James is to get your hands out of your pockets and keep them out, unless you are buying me a pint!"

Old Dave, standing nearby, laughed. "Where did you get that one from?" he said. "I can't remember saying that to you."

"You did!" I answered. "I think it must have been Monday, 10th August, 1959!"

Postscript

Bob died on 31st March, 2020 of sepsis. The majority of the work on this book was done in Tenerife many years ago with the exception of two chapters which he wrote later. I actually transcribed these chapters whilst he was in hospital so I was able to tell him that his book was complete.

Sorely missed and loved by all who knew him.

Brenda Betteridge